URBAN DICTIONARY

A dictionary of human interaction, defining slang, pop culture, and everyday urban life. A resource for parents trying to understand their kids, for language learners confused by real-world English—but most of all for your entertainment. A from-the-streets explanation of contemporary culture and language available online at www.urbandictionary.com, in the pages of this book, or from any nearby teenager.

ALSO FROM URBANDICTIONARY.COM
Mo' Urban Dictionary

New Edition

URBAN

DICTIONARY

FRESHEST STREET SLANG DEFINED

URBANDICTIONARY.COM,
COMPILED BY AARON PECKHAM

Andrews McMeel
PUBLISHING®

Andrews McMeel Publishing
a division of Andrews McMeel Universal
1130 Walnut Street, Kansas City, Missouri 64106

www.andrewsmcmeel.com

17 18 19 20 21 RR2 11 10 9 8 7 6

ISBN: 978-1-4494-0990-6

Library of Congress Control Number: 2011932644

Book design by Diane Marsh

ATTENTION: SCHOOLS AND BUSINESSES

SHOUT-OUT

Thanks to the millions of Urban
Dictionary authors who shared their
witty, offensive, and hilarious definitions
on urbandictionary.com over the last
twelve years.

at urbandictionary.com, definitions aren't written by professional lexicographers. They're written by everyday English speakers—the real authority on how language is used. For the last twelve years, their definitions have made urbandictionary.com the place to go to define any word, from abc sex to zomg. It's more than just slang—even words that appear in a regular dictionary are defined in Urban Dictionary.

I started Urban Dictionary in 1999 as a parody of the traditional dictionary, but it's grown to be more than a parody. It has developed a rebellious, opinionated, honest, anti-authoritarian personality, and the site grows with one new definition every 30 seconds.

Since 1999 authors have sent in over six million definitions. This book is the best of the best—definitions written by authors, approved by editors, enjoyed by readers, and now in print.

AARON PECKHAM

a crapella

Singing out loud while listening to music with your
headphones on. Whereas the singer gets the benefit of
the music, those unfortunate to be standing nearby are
subjected to an unaccompanied (and invariably crappy)
rendition of the song.

*I wish that guy would turn his iPod off—his a crapella version of
"Bohemian Rhapsody" is killing me.*

aarping

When an elderly person, such as your grandfather,
complains incessantly about nothing.

*Grandpa ruined another family dinner by aarping the whole time
about his bunions.*

abacadaba

To hurry up and get a multiple-choice test over with
because it is so hard that it is pointless to try to take it, or
because you don't care about the grade. From the format

of a multiple-choice test, where students fill in the lettered bubble of the correct answer.

Suze: How did you do on the test?

Regan: I just abacadabaed it.

abc gum
Stands for "already been chewed" gum. Typically found under desks in school.

I don't want your abc gum!

abc sex
Sex only on anniversaries, birthdays, and Christmas.

They've been married so long they only have abc sex.

academic bulimia
The process of learning or memorizing by rote, subsequently followed by the regurgitation of that knowledge onto an exam answer sheet. Just as with the serious eating disorder, this form of bulimia results in no real retention of substance. This term is frequently applied to describe a common practice of young medical students.

I can't remember anything that I learned last night. It's like I grabbed the answer sheet, puked out all the answers, and forgot everything immediately. I'd say that's academic bulimia.

acoustic shave
Shaving with a razor, not an electric shaver.

Andy: Hey man, do you use Norelco?

Jordan: No way. I shave acoustic!

act a fool

To act like a total idiot.

It is not a good idea to act a fool around your boss.

ADHD

Stands for attention deficit somethingk. Hey! I spelled "something" wrong. Ha-ha. Hey, look, a squirrel. Wait, what am I doing here again? Omigawd my elbow itches. Wonder what's on TV? I like Jennifer Lopez. I hate kumquats. I really love urbandictionar . . . where was I again?

Hey! I don't have ADH . . . (Loses interest, chases after a bird)

adverblasting

When a commercial is much louder than the program you were watching.

Man, I was watching NCIS, but I had to turn down my TV when the commercials came on because of damn adverblasting.

afterclap

That last person who keeps clapping after everyone else has stopped. Normally parents.

(Large chorus of clapping)

Mom: Did you hear little Billy's singing?

Aunt: Yes, his voice really stood out!

(Mom and Aunt are the last two clapping.)

aggro
Short for "aggravated." Crazy, wild.

The line was so long, and it was so hot, I started getting totally aggro.

aibohphobia
The irrational fear of palindromes (words that read the same forward and backward).

Dude 1: Hey, what's your name?

Dude 2: Bob.

Dude 1: AAAAAAAAAAH! (Runs and hides behind sofa)

Bob: Wow.

Dude 1: AAAAAAAAAAH! (Runs away and falls down stairs)

air jerk
Making a jerking-off motion with one's hand to express disgust, disinterest, or disbelief, while simultaneously rolling one's eyes.

I think she's pissed. She just gave me an air jerk and walked away.

air quotes
In conversation, the dual flexing of the index and middle finger of both hands to signify the presence of scare quotes. Used ad nauseam by "pretentious" and ostensibly "intelligent" university students to advertise their "superior morals" and "erudition."

Using air quotes in this example is, like, so "postmodern."

airplane mode

When someone cuts themselves off from the world by not logging on to Facebook or checking their cell phones. Usually occurs after a breakup or a rough workweek. Derived from the cell phone setting of the same name in which incoming messages or phone calls cannot be received.

Sarah went into airplane mode for three days after Charlie dumped her.

airport vultures

Passengers waiting to board a plane who stand around the boarding gate before a flight, regardless of where their seats are or when boarding actually is.

The flight attendant became so irritated with the airport vultures that the flight was abruptly canceled.

aisle salmon

Moving in the opposite direction of everyone else using the aisle. While they can be spotted in any type of aisle, they are frequently seen on airlines during loading and deplaning.

Did you see the aisle salmon trying to work his way back five rows to get a roller bag out of the overhead while everyone was trying to get off the plane?

alarm shock

The shock of having to wake up a lot earlier than you normally would due to school after summer vacation.

Alarm shock is such a drag! (Falls back asleep and misses bus)

alcohol

A substance found in beer (except American beer) and many other fine beverages that makes people excessively happy, sad, belligerent, or horny. It allows white people to dance and ugly people to get laid.

You wanna get with that hottie? You're gonna need to buy lots of alcohol!

alltheist

A person who tries to claim every religion out of fear of picking the wrong one. A typical alltheist believes in Jesus, Hindu gods, and even the Flying Spaghetti Monster.

Guy: I don't want to go to hell, so I'll just become an alltheist.

Girlfriend: Why am I even going out with you?

alt-tabbin'

The act of quickly switching the current application to something work appropriate when the boss walks in.

My boss almost caught me looking at porn at work. Good thing I was alt-tabbin'.

amateur hour

Something crappy. Something that seems amateurly put together.

Junior college is the amateur hour of higher education.

Amazonukkah

When Christmas really lasts eight days because the presents take longer to deliver from Amazon.com than anticipated by the purchaser. This is often caused by the reckless use of Super Saver Shipping on items that were bought on Christmas Eve. As a result, the presents are received in small amounts each day over an eight-day period, similar to Hanukkah.

Kid 1: Did you get everything you wanted for Christmas?

Kid 2: I dunno, we're celebrating Amazonukkah this year. My parents are real procrastinators.

amscray

Pig Latin for "scram," which means "leave."

(Mom and Dad are having sex when Little Johnny walks in.)

Johnny: Hi Mom! Hi Dad!

Dad: WTF?! AMSCRAY!

anchor

A person who can slow down an entire group. A person who requires constant help or attention from someone else.

What an anchor! She held up an entire line at the checkout for no reason.

and a half

Added to emphasize or exaggerate a quality or characteristic.

She is a bitch and a half!

and shit

A filler phrase used when you become too lazy to finish a sentence, or when you realize you just don't want to finish the sentence.

Girlfriend: What did you do last night?

Boyfriend: Oh, you know, we went to the bar and . . . you know, the bar and shit. Hey, how about that chick flick you always wanted to watch? Let's watch that.

and then I found five dollars

A phrase used at the end of a story that had really no point. Used at the end of boring stories to make them seem more interesting and worthwhile.

Yesterday, I went to the fridge and took out a yogurt but put it back and got an apple, instead . . . and then I found five dollars.

annivorcery

Anniversary of a divorce.

My parents' annivorcery was last month. Each of them celebrated with their new spouses.

antisocial networking

Using a social-networking website or service to connect to other people but never communicating with those people once they have been established as a connection.

We haven't spoken to Randy since high school. He added us as friends on Facebook but never responds to any of our messages. Talk about antisocial networking!

apocalypse sex

Thoughtless, careless sex happening right before a major disaster or possible ending of the world, without thought of consequences.

Figuring that this was the end of the world, I turned to the girl sitting next to me and said, "Why not?" We commenced passionate apocalypse sex; I just hoped that, this time, it was for real . . .

apple bottom

A female who has a large, round butt.

That girl's apple bottom is looking right.

approval from corporate

A term used to designate that the spouse in control of the household finances has given approval to make a large purchase.

Me: Did you get approval from corporate to purchase that $350 digital storage device?

Tim: Yes, with the proviso, "If you think we really need it."

arch douche

1. The title given to someone high on the corporate ladder, in a position of authority, etc., who is also a douchebag.

Jimmy is the arch douche of the accounting department.

2. A person who is not necessarily in authority but who is just a huge douchebag.

That guy is the fuckin' arch douche.

as you know

A phrase used when telling someone something they should already know, but in fact, the speaker knows they do not.

As you know, gang leadership is run from the prison infrastructure.

askhole

A person who asks many stupid, pointless, obnoxious questions.

God! Jimmy is such an askhole. He won't stop asking me about my favorite Teletubby, and I'm about to smash him in the grill, kid.

ass is grass

An expression foretelling a person's doom or demise. Originated from the fact that a murdered person's body decomposes and then provides fertilizer for grass, hence the "ass" becoming grass.

Your ass is grass if she gave you head while we were dating.

asstastic

1. A complimentary statement of one's posterior. Synonym for "bootylicious."

Gee, these pants make my rear end look asstastic!

2. A derogatory description for someone who excels at being an asshole. Synonym for "colossus assholus."

My ex was so asstastic he left me destitute.

attachment disorder

When a person forgets to attach a document to an email after explicitly stating that it is present.

Erin (RE: Look at this picture!!): You did not attach that picture on your last email.

Jeremy (Re: RE: Look at this picture!!!): I always forget to attach the picture before I hit send. I must have an attachment disorder.

attention spam

Any material or fodder that tends to destroy the attention span.

MTV spews pure attention spam all day, particularly by cutting cameras every three seconds.

attention whore

A person who craves attention so much that they will do anything to receive it. The type of attention (negative or positive) does not matter.

You're such a damn attention whore!

audience typing

When a person's typing abilities degrade when they type in front of others, leading to misspelled words, improper capitalization, and blushing.

Father: Put "Manchester United" into Google there for me.

Son: Sure. (Types "Manchetser UNited")

auto incorrect

When the auto-correct feature tries to correct your spelling but instead changes it to words that just don't make sense.

JR: Hey what time should I come over?

Victor: I dont know . . . Are you busty all evening?

Victor: I MEAN BUSY!! ARE YOU BUSY ALL EVENING! GOSH I HATE AUTO INCORRECT!

automagically

Something that happens automatically but that also has some mysterious magical element to it.

I installed Windows, and it screwed up my system automagically!

awesomeness

1. Exclamation of the immeasurable amount of awesome that something can produce.

Me: I found 50 bucks on the street! Let's go get wasted!!

You: Awesomeness!!

2. Something that qualifies as awesome.

Me: I won a free trip to Cancun!

You: That's awesomeness!

3. With sarcastic use, means that something is not awesome at all. A lower and calmer tone of voice is used, and is generally followed by derogatory physical action such as a shrug or eye rolling.

You: I'm so happy to be going with my family on vacation, where I can't party . . .

Me: Awesomeness . . . (Rolls eyes)

awkward arm

The arm that has nowhere to go when cuddling, spooning, or sleeping next to someone else. It usually leads to wishing arms could be pulled off and then put back on afterward.

(After trying to settle into a comfortable spooning position) Uh-oh, it's the return of AWKWARD ARM!

awkward turtle

The animal mascot of the awkward moment. When you're in an awkward moment, place your hands on top of each other, and spin your thumbs forward. This distracts people from the awkwardness of the moment.

Oh my god, so I was talking to Becky about STDs, and I forgot she had syphilis . . . it was mad awkward turtle.

babe paralysis

A temporary state whereby one's motor skills are severely impeded by the need to spontaneously interact with an extraordinarily attractive woman.

Jon suffered a bout of babe paralysis, rendering him a blabbering idiot when he turned and bumped into Olga, a Miss World finalist, at the airport in St. Petersburg.

baby

1. Term of endearment, usually used by people having sexual intercourse with one another.

When my girlfriend started calling my best friend "Baby," I knew it was over.

2. Exclamation, usually during sexual intercourse.

Oh baby! Yes!

3. The direct consequence of sexual intercourse.

How could something as good as sex have made this baby?

baby bump

The abdominal area of a pregnant woman.

Is she getting fatter, or is that a baby bump?

baby daddy

Short for "baby's daddy." The father of your child, whom you did not marry, and with whom you are not currently involved.

That man isn't my boyfriend; he's my baby daddy.

baby goggles

A phenomenon where the parents of an ugly baby think their baby is adorable and no one else does.

I think Nancy has baby goggles—that's got to be the ugliest baby I've ever seen!

baby mama

Short for "baby's mama." The mother of your child/ children, whom you did not marry, and with whom you are not currently involved.

Oh, her? She ain't nothing to me now, girl. She just my baby mama. So, can I get your number?

bachelor breakfast

Eating breakfast (or any meal) while standing at your kitchen counter instead of sitting at your kitchen table.

My dad drives my mom crazy eating his bachelor breakfast of burnt toast.

bachelor wash

A quick soap-free rinse of a recently used plate, cup, or utensil. Most useful for low-oil, water-based, or dry foods. Wiping with a paper towel will usually remove residual food particles missed by the bachelor wash.

I didn't want my date to think I was a pig, so I bachelor washed the dishes and tossed them in the cupboard.

backdoor braggart

A person who states a problem that they have with the express intention of letting everyone know how awesome they think they are, revealing their douchebaggery to all. Typically leads to eye rolls and general annoyance with the braggart.

Sarah: Lets go check out the new mall!

Lisa: Oh, I hate clothes shopping anymore. Since I've been working out I can never find anything that fits because my waist is too tiny and my tits are too big. Life is so unfair!

Sarah: You're such a backdoor braggart, Lisa. Go fuck yourself.

backseat surfer

Anyone who stands over your shoulder as you use the Internet, directing your Internet navigation.

No, I don't want to check out this totally amazing video on YouTube. Stop being a backseat surfer, douchebag.

baconify

To add bacon to otherwise baconless foods.

Baconify that burger for me, Cletus.

bad economy

An all-purpose excuse that people use during a recession to justify doing things that are below their usual standard. Often these things in reality have little or nothing to do with the economic circumstances.

Harry: You took your girlfriend to Applebee's on Valentine's Day? Pretty weak.

Larry: Whatever, man. I didn't have a choice. Bad economy.

Senator: Mr. Paulson, you really want to give the greedy, soulless bankers who caused this mess $700 billion with no strings attached?

Mr. Paulson: Hey guys, bad economy. Just do it.

Senator: Good point. I vote yes.

bad fuel day

The mood or feeling one experiences after having just filled his or her vehicle with $4.00+ per gallon gasoline. Usually consists of a sense of great economic despair, impending doom, anger, frustration, depression, and/or a combination of all the above.

Leave me alone. I'm having a bad fuel day!

badonkadonk

An extremely curvaceous female behind. Women who possess this feature usually have a small waist that violently explodes into a round and juicy posterior. Other characteristics are moderately wide hips and a large amount of booty cleavage.

Her badonkadonk made a brotha pop mad wheelies.

bagside

The side of a body where a gigantic purse or messenger bag is carried, creating an awkward barrier that prevents others from walking comfortably alongside.

I would hold your hand, Baby, but I don't want to get on your bagside.

Bale out

When someone's stress level explodes to an epic proportion and a five-minute f-bomb-laden tirade is unleashed on the unlucky soul who was in the wrong place at the wrong time—much like Christian Bale on the set of *Terminator Salvation.*

Pam was trying to study for her midterms in the library but the kid across the table kept tapping his pencil to his iPod. She Baled out and was suspended from the library for a week.

balls out

To exude tremendous effort; to try extremely hard.

I decided to slack off and get a B in the class, but Ross went balls out and got a 100 percent.

balls to the wall

Originally a military term for pushing maximum g-force in a jet fighter, as in pushing the ball of a throttle as high as it will go (virtually touching the wall of the dashboard). Fast; hectic; pushed to the limits.

We hit the road, balls to the wall, and got there in half the time.

bangin'

1. Describing people: sexy or attractive.

Nate: Did you check out dat ho'z dumps?

E: Fo' sheezy. Ain't they bangin', yo?

2. Describing things: great, wonderful, awesome, sweet, nice, dope, phat, tight.

Man, that car is bangin'!

bangover

Sore neck as a result of headbanging at a metal concert.

Zeb: How was the Meshuggah show last night, dude?

Cole: Ah, man it was sick! I got the worst fucking bangover, d00d.

banker's dozen

The opposite of a baker's dozen, where the customer receives thirteen of a product for the price of twelve. In a banker's dozen, the customer receives eleven of a product for the price of twelve.

Hector was surprised to find only eleven glasses in the set of twelve that received from the bank. Later, Hector learned that the bank offers a banker's dozen in their gifts and products, from which they steal one item.

barsexual

A college-age girl who kisses other girls in bars and clubs, usually for attention and the approval of men.

A bisexual girl kisses girls at home when no one's looking. A barsexual girl only kisses them in places that charge a cover.

bathroom stalking

Lurking just outside the bathroom door when another person is using it, usually accompanied by some attention-seeking noise or behavior, ensuring that that person will acknowledge your presence and hurry up.

I'll never be able to pee with you bathroom stalking me like that.

bats in the cave

Visible clumps of nose goblins, often found clinging to nasal hair.

You need to blow your nose. You got some serious bats in the cave!

BCG

Birth control glasses. Generally a military term that refers to the large, blocky glasses issued to military personnel who require the use of corrective lenses.

Man, these BCGs make me look like a complete idiot.

beard

Any opposite-sex escort taken to an event to give a homosexual person the appearance of being out on a date with a person of the opposite sex.

Half of the women on the red carpet at the movie premiere were not real dates, but beards.

beard goggles

When a beard-bearing individual is convinced that his facial hair looks great, regardless of how bad it may look to everyone else. Similar to beer goggles in that the more facial hair a person has, the better he thinks it looks.

Max: Wow, have you seen Dave's beard? It looks terrible. I don't know why he won't shave that thing.

Luis: It's because he has beard goggles right now, and in his mind it looks great.

bed gravity

An irresistible force that draws you back into bed, or toward any mattress, couch, or other soft horizontal surface. Usually stronger when one or more persons are already on said furniture.

Mom: Time to get up for school!

Son: Must! Fight! Bed gravity! . . . ZZZZZZZZZZZZ

bedgasm

A feeling of complete and utter euphoria that peaks when climbing into bed at the end of an eighteen-hour workday, a long road trip, or hours of extremely strenuous physical activity. Under perfect conditions, the physical release has been likened to that of an intense sexual experience.

It was a three-hour drive in the middle of the night, and I could barely stay awake. When I got home, I climbed under the covers and had a ten-minute bedgasm.

beer

The reason we get up in the morning and pass out at night.

Beer so good!

beer goggles

Phenomenon in which one's consumption of alcohol makes physically unattractive persons appear beautiful; summed up by the phrase "there are no ugly women at closing time."

When I took her to bed, she looked like Halle Berry. But when I woke up, she looked like Keith Richards! I must've had my beer goggles on.

beer tears

When, after a few drinks, someone becomes an unhappy drunk and begins to cry and shed tears about anything remotely bothering them. Subjects include ex-boyfriends, the inability to microwave Easy Mac, and spilling drinks on their shirt.

After I had three Natty Lights, I started regretting my last drunk hookup and started crying. My friends had to comfort me and wipe away my beer tears!

beer thirty

The time of day at which drinking a beer becomes necessary.

Hey, looks like it's beer thirty; better grab me a cold one.

beer under the bridge

When intoxicated individuals spar (either physically or verbally), and the next day agree to forget about it because they were drunk.

Nikki: I bet Joe was mad about me yelling and hanging up on him last night when I was wasted.

Kristin: He was blitzed, too. He said forget about it—it's beer under the bridge.

beerboarding

A controversial process of extracting otherwise-secret information from a friend or coworker by getting them drunk and thereby loosening their control of their tongue.

The guys at work took me out drinking last night. After quite a few beers and a lot of questions I finally let slip that I was going to be a father. What can I say? Beerboarding should be against the law.

best-behavior friend

Also known as BBF; a friend with whom you have very little in common, and so you act on your best behavior when they're around. They don't know the extent of your true character or transgressions because you lie to make yourself look good or innocent. A person with a best-behavior friendship may see the friendship as important or long-standing, and so lying about situations or leaving out key facts becomes common.

When Meg recounted last night to her best-behavior friend, Rachel, Meg neglected to mention that she had sex with her best friend's ex-boyfriend.

big in Japan

To pretend you are someone of stature somewhere else. Meaningless and not verifiable where you currently are.

Yeah, I am big in Japan.

big up

"Up" signifies elevation. Therefore, the term "big up"
literally means to elevate highly or to a superlative degree.

1. An expression of support or encouragement.

Big up on that excellent performance.

2. An expression of remembrance.

I want to big up everyone who has shown me support over the years.

biotch

1. A woman with unsavory character traits, often a negative
or belligerent attitude (i.e., a pain in the ass or a moody
bitch).

Yo, dawg, that girl ain't nothin' but a biotch.

2. A man whose abilities/character/mindset/emotional
responses are atypical of that which is generally associated
with being a man (i.e., acting like a girl, wimp, or
homosexual).

Yo, dawg, why you acting like such a biotch?

3. A nonoffensive colloquialism used to refer to a girl or a
woman with whom the speaker is associated. Also: beyatch,
biyatch, beyotch, biyotch, biznatch, bleyatch, bitch.

That's my biotch.

biPodding

Sharing a single set of headphones attached to one iPod. One person holds the iPod and takes the left earbud, the other takes the right earbud. Can be performed while moving.

Jane and Sarah block the whole sidewalk when they're biPodding down the street.

birthday brother/sister

Someone who shares your birthday (same day and same year). Even though you are not true siblings, this is a close bond.

Brady: Happy birthday, James.

James: Happy birthday to you, too, Birthday Brother.

bisexy

Appealing to both sexes.

My boyfriend isn't gay, but he thinks Brad Pitt is hot. Why? Because Brad Pitt is bisexy.

bitchen

The room in an urban apartment where both the bathroom and kitchen are located.

Trish's new apartment in Williamsburg has a bitchen.

BlackBerry jam

A human traffic jam that occurs in subway tunnels and bus stations. Caused by inconsiderate workaholics walking slowly while their noses are glued to their BlackBerry devices.

I was late for work because there was a BlackBerry jam getting out of the A train.

BlackBuried

Being inundated and exhausted, trying to be on top of all your email with your handheld mobile device.

Now that I have a BlackBerry, I feel obliged to attend to all my email day and night. I feel BlackBuried.

blacklight Barbie

A woman who appears much prettier in the blacklight at a party or club than she really is.

Seeing Whitney in the daylight, I realized she was a total blacklight Barbie.

bladdered

Drunk, as in with a full bladder. Tanked, hammered, stocious.

I was in the pub yesterday from 12 p.m. to 12 a.m. By the time I left I was bladdered.

blind transfer

When someone calls your office phone and you transfer them to a random number because you either can't find the correct number or you just don't feel like looking it up.

Coworker: Who just called?

You: I'm not really sure, but I totally just blind transferred him to someone in HR.

blinker beat

When the tick-tock of the blinkers syncs with the music playing on the car radio.

Dude, check it out, I got a blinker beat happening on this Jay-Z song.

blog

Short for "weblog." A meandering, blatantly uninteresting online diary that gives the author the illusion that people are interested in their stupid, pathetic life. Consists of such riveting entries as "homework sucks" and "I slept until noon today."

June 5: So, like, this morning Jenny called and wanted to know if I could come over, and Matt called, and Brian asked me to go to the mall with him. So I went to the mall and met up with some more of my friends and some guys started hitting on me and they were, like, so hot, too . . .

blootered

Intoxicated with liquor.

Had too many vodkas and got blootered pretty quickly.

bluetool

A person who wears a Bluetooth wireless earpiece everywhere they go to seem trendy and important. Places to spot bluetools include movie theaters, malls, restaurants, gyms, grocery stores, and cars.

Bluetool: Heyyy, how are you?

Megan: I'm great, and yourself?

Bluetool: Oh, sorry, Megan. I wasn't talking to you; I'm on a call. Bluetooth.

bluewalls

The female equivalent of blue balls.

Andre gave Christina bluewalls . . . and then he drove to Taco Bell to eat a grande meal.

BMS

Bitchy men syndrome. Male version of PMS.

Geez, that guy is so BMSing.

BOBFOC

Body off *Baywatch*, face off *Crimewatch*. A person who possesses a killer body but has a face that only a mother could love.

Check out that BOBFOC!

bogart

To keep something all for oneself, thus depriving anyone else of having any. A slang term derived from the last name of famous actor Humphrey Bogart because he often kept a cigarette in the corner of his mouth, seemingly never actually drawing on it or smoking it.

Don't bogart that blunt, man; pass that over here.

boink

A word that your parents use to describe sex to you, even when you are an adult.

Mom: Oh my lord, Jennifer! You're . . . you're not boinking him, are you?

Jennifer: Yes, Mom, he's my husband.

boner shock

When something happens that causes your boner to go into "shock," or go back into the flaccid stage.

That girl gave me boner shock when right before sex she said, "I always forget to take my birth control."

boo

1. Boyfriend or girlfriend.

Can you handle me? If you can't you ain't gonna be my boo.

2. Word used to scare people.

Guy 1: BOO!

Guy 2: Holy shit!

book Google

When you need to figure out something, so you look it up in a book—like in the olden times, when dinosaurs ruled the earth.

Guy 1: Quick! What's the definition of "callow"?

Guy 2: I don't know! My iPhone 4 doesn't get a signal here!

Guy 3: Book Google that shit!

boom shakalaka

The sound heard when someone makes an awesome slam dunk.

When Tim Duncan made that dunk, the announcers yelled in unison, "BOOM SHAKALAKA!!"

boot

To vomit.

I straight drank too much tequila, and now I have to boot!

booty call

A late-night summons—often made via telephone—to arrange clandestine sexual liaisons on an ad hoc basis.

The student's mother was ignorant of her son's booty calls.

booty grazing

The act of mass texting a generic message to members of the opposite sex, hoping to find a guaranteed hookup for the night. Often involves a very nonspecific message such as, "What are you up to tonight?" or "Want to meet up later?" The lack of personalization allows the same message to be sent to multiple contacts simultaneously.

Last night I went booty grazing and had to choose between three different hoes.

booty text

The lazy, low-commitment version of the booty call.

(Booty text from 555-5555) What are you doing? Wanna come over and sleep in my bed?

bored to debt

When you're so bored with life that you spend money to make your life seem more exciting.

Ben: What did you do this weekend, man?

Craig: I went shopping and bought a new 3-D TV and a PS3. Also went and got a dirt bike....

Ben: You already have a 60-inch LED flat panel, and you live in the middle of the city. Why did you go and get all that shit?

Craig: I dunno, nothin' to do . . . was bored to debt.

boregasm

Reaching the apex or climax of boredom. Filling one's capacity for boredom to the extreme boundary.

Riley: Dude, this class is so boring that I just boregasmed.

Annette: Oh yeah? Well I had three classes today . . . triple boregasm.

boss sandwich

An unfortunate cubicle configuration in which you find yourself sandwiched between two of your bosses.

I'm such a sad panda at work these days. I'm totally the lunchmeat in a major boss sandwich.

box lock

The female equivalent of a cock block.

I was hitting on that guy, but my girlfriend stepped in and totally box locked me.

boxset bully

Person who pushes you to watch huge quantities of their favorite TV show by offering to lend you the massive DVD box set. Applies to *Lost, The Wire, Band of Brothers, Battlestar Galactica, West Wing, Heroes, Dexter, Family Guy,* etc.

No, I've not seen The Wire. *I'm sure the script is superb, but I'm not willing to spend a week watching all sixty episodes, you boxset bully.*

boyfriend bomb

When a female you are interested in casually reveals that she has a boyfriend.

I was about to ask her out but then she dropped the boyfriend bomb.

bragplaining

When you complain about something for the sole purpose of bringing it up in conversation.

Abe: Man, I'm only getting 10MB/s download speed. Normally I get at least 15.

Ben: Quit bragplaining. We all know you're just bitching to show off.

brah

A term of affection used between males with fraternal bonds; brother, comrade.

Brah, you'd better stop picking your nose in front of Mr. Neidhart.

Brahs don't shake . . . brahs gotta hug!

brain bleach

What one might use to erase a particularly nasty image or memory.

Man, I just saw Olga in skin-tight canary-yellow stretch pants. I need to score me about five gallons of brain bleach!

brain boner

Something that strikes a chord in someone's thinking, creating a spur of "enlightenment" and stimulation in knowledge, especially in subjects like philosophy and logic.

John: Hey, have you seen that recent philosophical discussion on YouTube?

Peter: Yeah, it was so good it gave me a brain boner.

brain bucket

A motorcycle helmet.

You would have been hurt much worse in that accident if you hadn't been wearing your brain bucket.

brainspin

The inability to sleep because your mind can't slow down.

The Lost *finale gave me brainspin, and I wasn't able to sleep all night.*

brand dropping

Mentioning that you're wearing an expensive brand of clothing, using an expensive piece of technology, or bragging about other high-value items that you own.

Jon: Dude, watch it! If you spill that drink on my $350 Zegna shirt I'm gonna lose it.

Dave: Don't brand drop, Jon. No one cares what kind of shirt that is.

brand new

Dramatically improved behavior because of the presence of certain people.

Oh, she gonna act all brand new today because her friends are around! But last night she was all in my face!

break the seal

The point at which you first piss after you have been drinking your favorite alcoholic beverage. After this point, you will be pissing every ten minutes.

Damn, dude, I shouldn't have broken the seal.

break your crayons

Make you very upset or sad, or ruin your whole day.

Dude, don't worry about him; he's just tryin' to break your crayons. Just let it slide.

breakup buddy

A person who helps you make the right decision to break up. They give you an objective opinion of how bad the person is for you and provide postbreakup support.

I was thinking of getting back together with Laura. Luckily I had Michele as a breakup buddy, and she talked me out of it.

brickberry

A term for the old, outdated phone you have to use when your current phone breaks.

It takes me ten minutes to type a text message on this brickberry now that my iPhone broke, but at least I get to play Snake.

bro favor

Based on the Spanish "por favor," bro favor is an act of goodwill asked of one's bro or homey. It can also be used in place of the word "please" when asking a bro for a favor.

Dude, I could really use $7 to buy this limited-edition copy of Spawn. *Do me a bro favor and spot me $7?*

brodak moment

A picture with only the guys.

The guys and I all passed out on the couch last night. It was a perfect brodak moment.

brodeo

A get-together or party where the attendance is predominantly male.

So many dudes got wasted at Lou's brodeo out in Idaho.

brodown

Boys' night out. Like a hoedown, but with your bros.

Sorry, Baby, it's a brodown tonight.

bromance

The complicated love and affection shared by two straight males.

Steve: Ah, Dave!! I can't believe you stole this first pressing of Aladdin Sane *from your record store for me. We were just talking about this the other night.*

Dave: No sweat, pal.

Steve: That is some full-on bromance. You're the man.

broner

When a fiercely heterosexual male achieves an erection in the company of one of his male friends. May occur while engaging in all-male activities that include feats of strength or displays of hyper-masculinity.

The way you creamed that linebacker gave me a total broner.

brown chicken, brown cow

An onomatopoeic imitation of the guitar riff commonly heard in 1970s porn movies.

Jim: Hey, where are Abby and Jake?

Tom: Brown chicken, brown cow.

brown out

Less intense than the experience of "blacking out" when drunk and not remembering portions (or all) of your night. Occurs when you don't remember something until someone brings it up.

I didn't even remember making out with Bryanne until J-Lo told me! I definitely had a brown out last night.

buffer guest

A buffer guest is a close friend that you invite to a party fifteen minutes before the rest of the guests are expected to arrive. This guest is meant to 1) make it seem like the party has already begun and good times are to be had and 2) make it less awkward in case someone you don't know particularly well arrives before everyone else.

Jona's my buffer guest in case Tim or Josh come over early, because I don't really have a lot in common with them.

buffer race

The race between the playback line and the buffer bar on an Internet video.

Damn, I can't hear a freakin' thing this guy's saying. It keeps skipping because of the damn buffer race.

bullshit bingo

A game played during large corporate meetings. Players write down management words like "out-of-the-box thinking," "synergy," and "streamlining" on a 5 x 5 bingo card. When a word or phrase is used during the meeting, check the box. When you get five in a row, shout "bullshit bingo!" and win.

Company big shot fancy pants: And that is why this merger is going to benefit shareholder value by creating value-driven content.

You: BULLSHIT BINGO!

Company big shot fancy pants: You're fired!

bumper sticker activism

To tell the world what you think and what they should be doing by plastering your car with bumper stickers.

Jim: That "Keep Tahoe Blue" sticker is really making me wonder how to keep Tahoe blue.

Mike: Too bad the sticker's on a Ford Expedition, and keeping Tahoe blue involves reducing emissions.

bumpin'

Music when played at a high volume.

Yo, dude, that new stereo system of yours is bumpin'!

bunny boiler

After a breakup, the person who seeks revenge by stalking or harassment. From Glenn Close's character in *Fatal Attraction*, who boils her ex's pet rabbit.

I can't believe Kate. After we broke up she keeps ringing my place and hanging up when I answer. She turned into a real bunny boiler!

bus surfing

Riding a bus by standing in the aisle like a surfer, standing for as long as possible without touching anything (seats, poles, people) for support.

On the way home last night I was bus surfing for a full three minutes!

business buzzed

An acceptable level of intoxication for business situations.

We were slammed with TPS reports so we decided to crack open a couple beers and get business buzzed.

business provocative

Attire intended to provoke sexual arousal or attention in the workplace.

Sara's ruffle skirt is rather business provocative.

business shower

An intimate shower taken between two persons solely for the purpose of saving time, completely devoid of any sexual connotation.

Troy: Oh, shit, my alarm didn't go off!

Keenan: Shit, I have to be at work in twenty minutes.

Troy: We'll just have to shower together.

Keenan: Hey, man, that's gross.

Troy: Nah, it's cool. It'll be a business shower.

Keenan: Aight, dog.

butt billboard

Blatant advertising on the rump of a pair of girl's shorts or sweatpants. Synonym for "ass billboard."

She was standing there in the mall, in plain view, wearing a butt billboard that said "Nasty."

butt dial

When your cell phone accidentally calls someone you did not mean to while on your person.

I called her a fucktard. She heard 'cause my phone butt dialed her.

butt hurt

Easily offended, taking something too personally.

Jenny tries to hide her low self-esteem by being cocky, but when Joe tells her she's ugly, Jenny gets butt hurt.

butter face

A girl who is hot, except for her ("but her," hence "butter") face.

Kate is a real butter face.

butterfaith

A girl who is fun, intelligent, beautiful, perfect in every way . . . except she's devoutly religious.

If not for the whole going to church and not eating meat on Fridays thing, Jenny would be perfect. Too bad she's a butterfaith.

buysexual

Someone who gets turned on by, or derives sexual pleasure from, shopping, or being taken shopping.

Chad: I say, I do believe Edward took Muffy out shopping for jewelry this past weekend, at the conclusion of which she did give up the booty.

Sheldon: Mmm, QUITE the buysexual, wouldn't you say?

C

cactus legs
The feeling on a woman's legs after not having shaved.

I got cactus legs. I haven't shaved in a week!

California car pool
Traveling in a group where each member has their own car—rolling in an entourage.

Three office workers took three cars to lunch, executing a California car pool.

California stop
The act of slowing down but not fully stopping while driving. Applies mostly to right-hand turns at stop signs.

Sarah got a ticket for making a California stop when turning right at the intersection.

camel toe

Crotch cleavage (especially on a woman) that is visible through tight clothing.

Did you see that girl in spandex? She had serious camel toe going on.

Canadian refrigerator

A pile of snow in a cold winter where food or beverages can be stored. Great for parties.

Geoff: Are we out of Molson Canadian?

Robin: There's plenty in the Canadian refrigerator.

cankles

The area in affected female legs where the calf meets the foot in an abrupt, nontapering terminus. Worsened by weight gain and improved in appearance only by boots.

If I didn't have cankles, I might be able to wear those Prada loafers with my capri pants.

caps lock voice

When a normally calm person has to raise their voice and use an authoritative tone. It is equivalent to using the caps lock key in the digital world.

Chris was being run over at work, so Jason told him it was time to turn on his caps lock voice.

caraoke

Singing along with music in a car, especially loudly and passionately.

That long road trip felt a lot shorter because of the caraoke.

carb coma

The sleepy feeling after eating a large meal composed chiefly of carbohydrates, whether in the form of rice, noodles, or bread.

Dude, I was totally dozing at the office after that giant serving of chow mein for lunch. Total carb coma.

carbon cockprint

The amount of CO_2 and greenhouse gases released by a man in search of sexual gratification.

You're going all the way to Manchester to shag that bird? Your carbon cockprint must be massive!

carcolepsy

A condition affecting buddies on a trip who fall asleep as soon as the car starts moving, providing no company or driving help.

Joe slept the whole way here. I think he suffers from carcolepsy.

career veneer

The thin layer of potential for career advancement, or increase in pay and future opportunities that an employer paints on your job to convince you that the future holds something more than you are currently experiencing.

I had my first year appraisal at the McDonald's today. They painted a bit of a career veneer over the last year.

cash chucker

Derogatory term for an exceptionally rich person.

It seems like more and more of these cash chuckers are moving into the neighborhood these days.

Cashmas

The primary holiday celebrated in capitalist cultures. A celebration of materialism in which people attempt to flatter or impress relatives, friends, and acquaintances with the extent of their purchasing power. Also "$mas."

In the United States, where the holiday is most actively observed, Cashmas traditionally begins on "Black Friday," the day following Thanksgiving. Holiday observations traditionally end on January

Jodi spent fourteen hours at the mall in celebration of $mas.

catch feelings

To fall in love with someone at an inappropriate time or mistake a repeated hookup for a serious relationship.

I broke it off when she caught feelings and asked me to stop hooking up with her friends.

celebrity lay

A specific celebrity you and your significant other mutually agreed that it would be okay to have sex with should the two of you ever meet in public and have a one-night stand.

My husband won't mind. Kiefer Sutherland is my celebrity lay.

cell phone samba

The erratic movements of a person trying to get better cell phone service.

The other day, a man ran into me while doing the cell phone samba in the grocery store.

cellfish

Word used to describe an individual who talks on his or her cell phone even when doing so is rude or inconsiderate of other people.

Can't you stop talking on the phone while ordering your Happy Meal? It's cellfish.

cellular isolation

Occurs when two people are partitioned by one party's separate conversation via phone call or text message using a cellular device.

The conversation was quite riveting until Becky initiated cellular isolation by sexting for the remainder of the evening.

century club

A legendary club you become a member of by drinking 100 beer shots in 100 minutes. This club doesn't have meetings or anything; you just use it to impress frat buddies, hoes, or practically anyone who admires feats of great alcohol consumption.

If you can't join the century club twice in one night, you're a pathetic lightweight.

chairdrobe

The art of piling clothes on a chair to be used in place of a closet or dresser.

I searched through my chairdrobe to find my outfit for work.

cheappuccino

Any of the wide variety of flavored coffee drinks offered at convenience stores. They can be purchased for less than half the price of a Starbucks cappuccino.

Let's stop by the store for some cheappuccinos tonight. It's gonna be cold, and all I've got is $1.25 in my wallet.

cheat chain

When one kid copies answers from a smart kid in class, then another kid copies from them, and then someone copies off the kid who copied off the kid who copied from the smart kid. Eventually everyone in the cheat chain has the smart kid's answers. Ideal for desks set in rows.

I'm really glad we organized that cheat chain on Friday. I actually have a chance of not failing.

check my spam

Checking one's email though one is certain one has received no important communication. Compulsively and frequently checking one's email when one is not expecting an important message.

Between friends in a cybercafe:

Brantley: Hey, could you hurry up so I can get on and check my email?

Tim: Who are you kidding, little bro? You know all your email buddies have dropped you like a brick!

Brantley: Yeah, I gotta check my spam—vamoose!

check your totem

A reference from the movie *Inception* that suggests that a person should examine their totem (small personal object) in order to determine whether they are in reality or in delusional dreamland. Intended to be used sarcastically.

Douchebag: I swear every girl in that club wanted me.

Smugster: Go check your totem.

check your vitals

To check your email and Facebook.

Shaina: Hey, wanna go get something to eat?

Jordi: Sure, but lemme finish checkin' my vitals first.

chedda

Short for "cheddar." Cash money, scrilla.

I'm piled high in the chedda.

cheesin'

Walkin' around with a huge smile on your face—like when someone is taking a picture and they tell you to "Say cheese!"

That dude's cheesin'! Wonder why he's so happy.

cheet

The orange dust that coats your fingers and lips after eating Cheetos.

I know you've been eating my Cheetos again—you've got cheet all over your clothes!

chew toy

The person you have or will have carnal relations with, but never a serious relationship.

Do you like my chew toy for the night? I met him on the dance floor.

child supervision

When an older person, especially a parent, needs a tech-savvy kid to help them with computers or other electronic devices.

Jimmy, could you send your kid over to help me with my Facebook? I'm afraid I might get a virus without some child supervision.

chillaxin'

A mixture of "chillin'" and "relaxin.'"

I'm not doing anything. I'm just sittin' on the couch chillaxin'.

chin strap

A patch of hair grown on the chin that looks like a chin strap for a football helmet. Similar to a goatee.

Jimmy was so proud because, after months of practice, he was finally able to grow and perfect his chin strap.

chiptease

When you buy a bag of chips thinking that it will be full of chips but when you open the bag it's barely full.

I bought a bag of chips out of the vending machine and there were only 5 chips in the bag. What a chiptease!

choreplay

When a woman is turned on by the sight of her husband/boyfriend/partner doing regular household chores.

Last night, it was all about choreplay. I was all, "OH YEAH, fold that laundry. Oh yes, just like that! In half, and then in half again. OHHH!"

Christmas bogus

Receiving nothing from your employer for Christmas.

Once again, my cheap boss gave us all a Christmas bogus.

Christmas syndrome

When you are looking forward to something constantly, to the point of obsession, causing the actual event to seem short and dull in comparison.

Oh, he's been counting down the days since July, and has come down with a bad case of Christmas syndrome.

chronoptimist

A person who always underestimates the time necessary to do something or get somewhere.

Lisa: Hey, Cindy, you know my parents are expecting us in twenty minutes.

Cindy: No problem. I just have to wash the dishes, take a shower, do my hair, walk the dog, and then I'm all good to go. See you in fifteen.

Lisa: You are such a chronoptimist! I'll see you in forty-five.

chunder

Vomit; generally chunky in nature.

He hurled in my car and now there's a lake of chunder in the backseat.

citation needed

A disclaimer for any time you quote something from Wikipedia as fact. Acknowledges that it isn't the world's most "reliable" source, but it's still good enough for you to use.

Drew: I heard the old Red Ranger from Mighty Morphin' Power Rangers *is gay, citation needed.*

Cody: Yeah, I heard that elephant populations have tripled in three years, citation needed.

Clark Kent job

Your day job, or a job that helps pay the bills but is not what you really want to do.

What's your Clark Kent job?

clicktease

When a website or website link leads you to believe you will be seeing pornography or some other sexual material, when in fact the offer is false or misleading.

Man, I thought that email was totally my ticket to free porn, but it ended just being home loans and pay sites! What a clicktease!

clutch

1. Great, essential, and potent rolled into a single word. Used to describe an action.

Pulling that move on Jenna was clutch.

2. Ability to perform under pressure.

In the last few seconds of a close game, only a player with clutch can lead the team to victory.

clutch oven

To fart in a car full of people while cranking the heat for maximum effectiveness.

Mike was driving us to Jake's party and he farted, trapping us in his clutch oven.

cobra yawn

The involuntary spraying of saliva while yawning. Much like the venom spray from a cobra. In most cases the yawner doesn't realized it has happened, only finding the aftermath once the yawn is over.

I just cobra yawned all over my keyboard five minutes prior to writing this definition.

cockblocalypse

When you're out at the bar and you get cockblocked so bad it's like the end of the world as you know it.

Miller: What's up with Gurpreet?

Steve: Oh, last night, Trong brought the cockblocalypse upon him.

cockblocked by Steve Jobs
When the opposite sex makes eye contact with you, then plugs into their iPod as a defense mechanism to prevent you from making a move.

Josh: I saw this girl on the bus and was going to hit on her, then she busted out her iPod.

Sam: Aw man, you got cockblocked by Steve Jobs.

COD diet
When you lose a lot of weight due to missing meals because you play too much Call of Duty.

Guy 1: Dude, have you lost weight?

Guy 2: Yeah. After Black Ops came out, I went back on the COD diet.

cognitus interruptus
A disruption of the normal thought process, usually by an external distraction. This occurs most often at times when mental focus is a necessity. Cognitus interruptus sometimes leads to procrastination, leading to further cognitus interruptus, thereby creating a cycle.

Constant cognitus interruptus in my classes kept me from passing finals.

coin wanking

The act of jangling change held in a suit trouser pocket. Usually performed by male office workers while standing and chatting with colleagues.

Jeff and Greg stand and chat, simultaneously coin wanking, caressing and fondling the change in their pockets.

coincidance

What happens in a musical when random strangers in a scene bust into an intricately choreographed number.

I loved the coincidance in (500) Days of Summer. *Who knew Joseph Gordon-Levitt could dance like that?*

coitus hiatus

To have a break from sex.

I'm not sexually frustrated; my man parts are simply on coitus hiatus.

cold finger

Similar to cold shoulder, a cold finger is ignoring someone's text or Facebook message—usually when their comment is pointless or uncalled for.

FB status: Man, I just got called into work for another 16 hour weekend shift.

Tool: Lol, I never work weekends lol (The cold finger is appropriate here.)

cold jerky

Suddenly and altogether stopping a perpetual masturbation habit. Can apply to male or female.

The only way to stop was to go cold jerky.

combat nap

That five- to ten-minute nap that you have to take when your body is completely exhausted and your mind is overstressed. Happens if you want it or not, and you usually wake up feeling like you've had a full night's rest.

Joe pulled watch on my post so I could grab a combat nap.

coming out of the cupboard

Popular or unpopular people's disclosure of their secret obsession for Harry Potter. Comes from the well-known phrase "coming out of the closet," which refers to a person revealing that they are gay/lesbian. The "closet" part is replaced by "cupboard," because Harry Potter lived in the "cupboard under the stairs" in the beginning of the book series.

Now that Harry Potter has gone so mainstream, I guess it's safe to finally come out of the cupboard.

compunicate

When you are in the same room with someone, each on separate computers, and you talk via Instant Messenger instead of speaking to them out loud, in person.

Even though they are sitting right next to each other, Jesse and Justin only compunicate when they have to tell each other something.

computer-face

To squint and kind of frown as you look at your computer to give the illusion that you are in fact very busy analyzing something vital to your work.

Often used in conjunction with paper shuffling and calling numbers that you know won't answer, then acting really frustrated when you hang up so that it gives the impression you're chasing a very important account and have a lot on your plate already.

After I computer-faced Facebook for an hour this morning, I called a random number and talked to an older gentleman for twenty-seven minutes about the prospect of leasing his mineral rights until he realized he didn't own any mineral rights, so I hung up and went back to computer-facing a New York Times *article about fashion week.*

condomonium

Trouble finding a condom.

It was condomonium when I looked in my wallet for protection.

congreenient

Word used to describe the practice of recycling, or being green, only when convenient.

I would have recycled my Fiji water bottle, but my plastic bin was full. I guess I'm just congreenient.

connectile dysfunction (CD)

The inability to gain or maintain an Internet connection. The inability to print, email, or get to the Internet.

My computer had connectile dysfunction (CD) yesterday, so I couldn't check my email.

conversational blue balls

When someone brings up a topic when talking but immediately drops it and refuses to switch back to the dropped topic.

Annie: Goodness, did you hear about what happened?

Rita: What happened?

Annie: Anyways, I'm gonna go.

Rita: Wait, what happened?

Annie: Oh, don't worry about it.

cookie duster

A full mustache capable of dusting the tops of cookies.

Check out the cookie duster on Brad!

cool story bro

Phrase used sarcastically to express a lack of interest in what the other person is saying.

Person 1: I think people who listen to metal are mindless idiots.

Person 2: Cool story bro.

cosplay

Literally "costume play." Dressing up and pretending to be a fictional character (usually a sci-fi, comic book, or anime character).

There are anime cosplay conventions around the world.

couching distance

The distance one can reach without leaving the couch.

I can't reach the remote control because it's not in couching distance.

courier new

What you do to add multiple pages to your papers if your professor doesn't have a font requirement and you can't think of anything else to write.

Yo, man, I said fuck it and courier newed that research paper.

courtesy fart

When someone accidentally farts and is embarrassed, you should, if you have one ready, let one fly, as well. This is an opportune time for you to release since then the two fart smells will interfere and no one will discover how unbelievably nasty your ass is.

Boris farted as he bent over to pick up his shuttlecock at the badminton tournament. Shung Fe felt so bad for him that he offered up a courtesy fart. Unfortunately, Shung Fe's rice and egg-noodle fart was no competition for the liverwurst and vodka fart from Boris, and everyone had to leave the court for fifteen minutes.

courtesy wash

The common practice of men after using a public restroom in which, instead of actually washing their hands, they simply dampen them under the sink and then dry them on their pants or a paper towel, thus giving the illusion that they did in fact wash their hands.

She ragged on you about washing your hands? Why didn't you do a courtesy wash?

craptacular

Spectacularly crappy.

Your home movies are craptacular, Chris.

critical ass

The stage in fat accumulation when fabric can no longer contain the enormity of one's buttocks.

Jesus, I can't zip up these jeans anymore—I've reached critical ass!

crop dusting

Farting while walking; walking while farting.

I crop dusted my way down the aisle at the grocery store.

cruiser spooning

The act of parking two police cruisers with the drivers' sides adjacent so that the officers can converse through the open windows.

Better slow down, the po-po are cruiser spooning in the parking lot ahead.

crunk

1. A state of high energy, as described by rapper Lil Jon & the East Side Boyz. Southern word for getting rowdy, out of control, having fun, partying, going crazy.

We about to get crunk up in this piece!

2. Getting a little crazy, a little drunk.

I'm planning on gettin' crunk tonight.

cubicle coma

When you wake up and feel energized, but as soon as you enter the workplace a wave of exhaustion runs over you, and you have trouble staying awake for the rest of your workday. Amazingly, once you leave the hellish work atmosphere, you suddenly feel energized and ready to run a marathon.

As soon as I sat down at my desk this morning, cubicle coma came over me and I immediately passed out. An IV coffee drip could not pull me out of it; but as soon as I walked out to go home, I felt like I could do an Ironman.

cubicle farm

Monotonous office environment characterized by white-collar slaves wasting their lives in pseudo-offices with four-foot walls while slowly morphing into zombies.

After three hours in the cubicle farm, I could feel my brain turning into a mushy mass of rotten puddinglike material.

cuddle call

A phone call (or a text) to arrange an immediate cuddle date. Not a booty call but similar in the call-for-satisfaction nature of the behavior.

Nate: Hey, Baby. What's going on?

Treena: Hi. Cuddle call?

Nate: See you in ten minutes.

cupcaking

Flirting or being flirtatious.

Ayyo, stop cupcaking wit that ugly ass ho.

curb shame

Embarrassment at waiting on the curb obediently as other pedestrians ignore the "don't walk" signal in the absence of traffic.

I couldn't stand the curb shame any longer, so I crossed with everyone else, even though I needed a break from running all around town.

cyberchondriac

Someone who spends their time searching medical websites for diseases they convince themselves they actually have. Similar to a hypochondriac.

Sam: Then I went on this website and found out that I actually have diabetes AND chronic fatigue!

Billy: Dude . . . you're a cyberchondriac.

daddy badge

Vomit or snot from a baby found around the upper chest or shoulders of their father, which shows the world that he is a parent.

Nice shirt, Pete, was the daddy badge an optional extra?

dap

The knocking of fists together as a greeting or form of respect.

He gave me a dap when we greeted.

darth breather

A person who breathes so loud they sound like Darth Vader, especially in quiet places.

Michael: Man! I couldn't complete my exam yesterday.

Jeffrey: Why? Was it that hard?

Michael: No, but there was a darth breather behind me.

dead text

A text that is received too long after it's sent so you are no longer obligated to reply to it.

I received a message from my friend the morning after it was sent, asking if I was still up; so I decided not to reply because it was a dead text.

deface

To remove a friendship from Facebook after either accidentally adding him/her as a friend or reconsidering later.

Yeah, there was this guy in my network who added me. I thought he looked okay, but his updates were really cramping my news feed, so I had to deface him.

defensive eating

Strategically consuming food for the sole purpose of preventing others from getting it.

Matt's mother-in-law unexpectedly arrived with a delicious dinner immediately after Matt finished a 12-inch sub. In order to prevent his wife from getting the surprise meal, he used defensive eating to consume the additional food.

deja boo

Wearing the same old Halloween costume to parties, year after year.

It's like deja boo all over again when I see Amelia wearing the naughty nurse costume.

designated drunk

Responsible partiers choose a designated driver to drive during a night of debauchery. The designated drunk is chosen by the driver. The designated drunk assumes responsibility for all drink offers given to the driver, including toasts, shots, and drinking competitions.

Random drunk: Hey dude! Come have a shot with me!

Designated driver: Gary, you're DD. Take that shot for me.

Gary: All right.

designated texter

A passenger who reads and replies to any and all text messages received on the driver's phone, allowing the driver to focus on the road and not hit anything or get pulled over for reckless driving.

Guy 1: Whoa, I almost hit that telephone pole back there. Dude, you should be my designated texter.

Guy 2: Yeah, no problem, bro.

destinesia

When you get to where you were intending to go, you forget why you were going there in the first place. Not to be confused with being stoned, destinesia often occurs during working hours, and is the cause of much frustration.

John ran down the stairs to the dry storage and walk-in, but when he got there he couldn't remember what he needed. Consequently, he had to run back upstairs to the kitchen, and look at his prep list again. Damn you, destinesia!

DFL

Dead fuckin' last.

Frank just got a DFL at the race.

dick flick

The testosterone-driven opposite of a "chick flick." Generally contains lots of car chases, explosions, and boobs.

Dave, wanna get some cold ones and watch Platoon? *I'm in the mood for a dick flick.*

dick inches

Arbitrary (and usually incorrect) units of measurement used mostly by males. Derives from men overestimating their penis size, but the term is usually used when overestimating nonpenis measurements. Dick inches are much shorter than actual inches. Hence a guy can claim to have a 9-inch penis when it is actually closer to 5 or 6 inches.

Fellow 1: Finally! There's a parking spot!

Fellow 2: No way, man . . . You can't park within 30 feet of a stop sign.

Fellow 1: There's plenty of room.

Fellow 2: Yeah, only if you're measuring in dick inches.

dick offset

Similar to a carbon offset. Involves bringing a girl/girls to a party to increase your chances of getting in by negating the effect of another guy in the place.

Guy 1: Damn, this party is a real sausage fest; we're never getting in.

Guy 2: Relax, I brought Alesia and Watermelondrea as dick offsets.

diet whoopass

A can of whoopass requiring less energy and only three calories per serving. What you open up when you're too weak to open up a regular can of whoopass on someone.

Hell, I'm tired—I only got diet whoopass left.

ding dong ditch

To ring a random person's doorbell and run.

I played ding dong ditch for hours until I got caught.

dinner badge

Dried stains of food (kebab juice, curry sauce, gravy) all over your shirt from messy eating.

That's an impressive dinner badge you've got there. What did you eat, pizza?

dip out

To leave a party or someone's house without them knowing. Could be sneaking out; or just plain leaving.

Don't mean to trip out, but bitch, I'm 'bout to dip out.

directionally challenged

Having difficulty determining right from left. People who are directionally challenged often prefer visual markers when following directions and may have great difficulty reading maps and/or driving while listening to directions.

Woman: You just turned left instead of right.

Man: I'm sorry, I'm directionally challenged.

disco nap

Sleeping when you've got something going on later that you need to be awake for.

I was about to go to the club, but I needed a disco nap to feel refreshed.

dish envy

Sudden, intense longing and regret derived from watching a particularly appetizing dish being delivered to a nearby table, and realizing that one has made an inferior menu selection.

Hank was eagerly anticipating his scallops when the waiter brought the stuffed pork chops to the man at the table next to him. Unable to avert his gaze, Hank began to feel the anguish of dish envy.

Disneyfication

The act of taming the world to make it all safe, clean, and completely similar to a theme park. To remove the sharp edges and darkness that is life.

NYC suffered from Disneyfication under Rudy, and now is as boring as any small town USA.

do I smell popcorn?

Phrase uttered when you have passed a particularly pungent bubble of gas that you are so proud of you want everyone to take a deep whiff.

We all knew we were in trouble when Amber asked, "Do I smell popcorn?" We just didn't know that it was lethal.

do you like hobbies?

Something you say during an awkward pause in conversation in attempt to start conversation. However, this will just make the conversation more awkward and draw attention to the pause.

Person 1: Yeah, that was by far the best Family Guy *episode ever.*

Person 2: Yeah, for sure.

Person 1: ...

Person 2: ...

Person 1: So ... do you like hobbies?

don't cross the streams

What you tell two people peeing at urinals next to each other to save them from untimely death, in reference to crossing the streams in *Ghostbusters.*

Whoa! Watch out! Don't cross the streams!

don't take this the wrong way, but . . .

What you say to someone right before you say something that can only be taken one way: badly.

Don't take this the wrong way, but every time you enter the room it smells like someone smeared shit all over my face.

dooced

Losing your job for something you wrote in your online blog, journal, website, etc.

Did you hear Mary got fired yesterday for writing about her boss in her blog? Yeah, she got dooced.

doppelbangers

A person who has sexual intercourse with someone who looks identical to them but is not related.

OMG, they both have bowl cuts and are 6 feet tall. TOTAL doppelbangers.

dork

1. An individual who is keenly interested in and good at mathematics, science, and technology, and applies mathematical and scientific principles to everyday occurrences while being lovable and very personable, often having many friends due to wittiness, and often loves video games. Not to be confused with "nerd," "geek," or "dweeb."

Dork: Wow, that lightbulb that's flickering in a seemingly random fashion is actually occurring as such due to a capacitance built up on one side of the tungsten filament until it discharges, sending electrical flow through the tungsten, causing photonic emission through heated excitation, which then dissipates as you get farther from the lightbulb, according to inverse square law.

Girlfriend who is also a dork: You're right, you dork. Shut up and kiss me. You're so cute.

2. Someone who is a loser, clumsy, stupid, and/or has no common sense.

You can be a total dork at times. I don't know why I hang out with you.

double freeture

When you pay for one movie at the cinema but sneak into a second flick once the first one is done.

I went to see Hancock, *and when it was over I decided to treat myself to a double freeture and snuck in to watch* Wall-E.

double-chipping

When a houseguest reaches into a bag of chips and eats some, then licks all over their hands, then reaches into the bag and eats some more chips.

Me and a buddy were eating Hot Cheetos, but he kept double-chipping, so I let him have the rest.

douchebaguette

A female douchebag.

Just look at her pompous gait . . . what a douchebaguette!

Dr. Google

A person medically qualified by Google's search engine to diagnose symptoms of sickness.

My son has dengue fever. That's what Dr. Google told me.

Dracula sneeze

Holding your arm up over your face in a position similar to Dracula holding up his cape, then sneezing into your elbow.

Due to the H1N1 swine flu pandemic, the Centers for Disease Control recommends using the Dracula sneeze technique to avoid spreading germs.

drafternoon

Any time after 12 p.m. to start pouring cold ones.

My morning has sucked a fat one. I can't wait for the drafternoon.

dragging balls

Taking too much time to complete a task; procrastinating; never ending.

(Office setting. Coworkers hunched over desks.)

Gil: Fuck! It's only 10 a.m.?

Juan: Yep. Today is dragging balls.

driver's arm

A left arm that is tanner (or redder) than the right because it's been hanging out the window.

Dude 1: Hey, man, I took a trip to LA last weekend. . . .

Dude 2: Yeah, man, I know . . . you've got major driver's arm!

driving finger

Your middle finger. Usually refers to the one on the left hand so it can be displayed out the driver's side window to comment on another driver's behavior.

Your driving finger is the longest finger.

drop science

To educate (or "school") someone or show off what you know, usually in rap.

Yo' rhymes are weak. Sit back and watch me drop science on yo' ass.

drum driving

While you are driving and listening to music, you bang on the steering wheel as if it were a drum set.

Would you please pay attention to the road and stop drum driving?!

drunken immunity

Complete disregard on the part of a friend, girlfriend, or ex-girlfriend for any minor stupid thing you said or did while drunk (e.g., drunk texting, drunk calling, drunken Facebook status updates, drunken confession, etc.).

Ex-girlfriend: We broke up two days ago. Why did you call me at 3 a.m. for a booty call?

You: I plead drunken immunity.

DTR

Acronym for "define the relationship." When two people discuss their mutual understanding of a romantic relationship (casual dating, serious boyfriend, etc.).

Friend 1: Have you DTR'ed yet?

Friend 2: I dunno what we are. I guess we gotta do a little DTR'ing tonight.

dub

1. Abbreviation for the letter "W."

I drive a V. dub.

2. Twenty dollars.

That CD player costs two dubs.

3. Twenty dollars' worth of anything, especially narcotics.

Lemme get a dub; I gotta get high.

4. Plural: 20-inch rims on tires.

I got my Escalade rollin' on dubs.

5. The art of making a remix, especially a reggae song, in which the lyrics are all or partially removed and the focus is placed on the drum track and the bass. Generally used as a name for any remix to any song.

Lee "Scratch" Perry is the master of the traditional reggae dub, especially his work with Sir Robert Nesta Marley.

duckface

A term used to describe the face made if you push your lips together in a combination of a pout and a pucker, giving the impression you have larger cheekbones and bigger lips.

Oh Christ, look at that horrific duckface.

dudevorce

When two male best friends officially end their friendship over a lame disagreement, usually concerning a girl.

Spencer and Brody got a dudevorce over Lauren.

dutch oven

To fart under the covers and then pull them over your own or someone else's head.

Chris fainted when I gave him a dutch oven.

dungeon tan

The pale skin of a person who plays too much Xbox and doesn't get any sunlight.

Bryce: Yo, Tim hasn't come out in days.

Jess: Yep, he's playing Xbox, working on his dungeon tan.

earjacking

Eavesdropping on a conversation that you have no business hearing.

Bob totally earjacked my conversation with Susie, and now everyone knows I got a boob job.

early nerd special

Midnight showing on the day of release of a highly anticipated film, typically of the science-fiction/fantasy genre.

I'd like one adult ticket to the early nerd special of Harry Potter and the Deathly Hallows: Part 2.

Earth

God's reality TV show.

Earth gets good ratings on Uranus.

eat humble pie

To be forced to apologize or to admit a fault.

I caught Pierson in another lie, so he has to eat some humble pie.

eau d'ouche

The obnoxious, headache-inducing cologne cloud that surrounds a beefy, tight-Armani-shirt-wearing dude.

Ugh. Some big meathead just walked by wearing way too much eau d'ouche. I feel like I'm gonna puke.

econnoisseur

One who insists on the highest quality at the lowest price.

Being an econnoisseur, I bought the ten-dollar Chilean wine instead of the fifty-dollar French.

economic vegetarian

Only eating vegetables because you can't afford to buy meat.

He used to be an economic vegetarian, but then he got a better job and can afford to buy steak.

edgehog

A passenger on the bus who hogs the aisle seat.

I rode the bus with the ultimate edgehog! I had to squeeze my way to the window seat.

elbow tag

When in a theater with shared armrests, the act of carefully adjusting one's posture so that your arm touches the arm of the person next to you, but not so much that they move their arm away.

Jenna was pretty sure Mark still believed in cooties, so she got all giddy during their Ice Age: Dawn of the Dinosaurs *date when she won a game of elbow tag.*

electile dysfunction

The inability to become aroused over any of the choices for president put forth by either party during an election year.

Ike: Is anyone appealing to you in this year's presidential race?

Jason: Naa. . . . No one excites me. I think I'm suffering from electile dysfunction.

elevator circles

Walking awkwardly around a large elevator lobby after you press the button, because you don't know which elevator door to stand by.

At work yesterday, my boss walked by while I was doing my elevator circles, and now he thinks I'm crazy.

elevision

The act of people in an elevator staring up, uncomfortably, at the numbers as they light up when the car moves. Practiced out of nervousness.

When the elevator began moving, silence ensued as each person practiced their elevision.

email bail

Using email to back out on plans, dates, and even relationships.

He didn't want a confrontation, so he decided to email bail on the chick he promised to call last night.

email courier

An individual who approaches someone's desk or workstation in a work environment almost immediately after sending them an email, usually to confirm that the email has been received.

Bill: I just sent you an email. Did you get it?

Mike: Probably; I haven't checked.

Bill: Can you check?

Mike: Uh yeah, looks like I got it.

Bill: Thoughts?

Mike: My immediate thoughts are you're an email courier and a douchebag.

emotional dump

Unloading all of your emotional crap unmercifully onto one or more of your friends.

Jill called today and took the longest emotional dump on me.

engayed

The term to describe gay couples who have become engaged to get married.

Did you hear the news? Paul and Tom got engayed. I can't wait for their wedding!

enragement ring

A piece of jewelry, typically a ring, that is purchased for a girlfriend in an effort to make her happy after you have made her angry.

Kenny: Wow, your girlfriend is pretty pissed that you were out all night and didn't call her. What are you going to do?

Reese: Yeah, you're right, she's pretty mad. I might have to buy her an enragement ring to smooth things over.

eroticon

A sexually explicit animated icon used in chat conversations.

Pat really got me in trouble with my boss when he unleashed his new bukkake eroticons in our MSN chat while I was doing a presentation to a group of investors.

errorist

Someone who repeatedly makes mistakes. Says stuff he believes is true, but anyone with common sense can see he's wrong. A dumbass.

Bush is talking on TV again. What a fucking errorist.

establish a beachhead

Military term now used to describe the act of positioning oneself and one's crew at the front of the bar to ensure primo cocktail service and quality lay of the land.

Paul and Carl agreed to get to the bar early to establish a beachhead.

etm

Latin abbreviation for the literal translation of "and shit," specifically "et merda." Just like "etc." (and so forth), "i.e." (that is), and "e.g." (for example).

At the farmer's market I got tomatoes, cucumbers, radishes, etm.

evasive mumbling

Mumbling the answer to a question in hopes that the questioner won't hear or understand an answer that may get you in trouble.

When Mom asks about that broken plate, you better answer with some evasive mumbling.

ex with benefits

After a breakup of a couple, they remain close friends, and still practice some form of physical closeness. Can occur anytime after the breakup.

John: Mary, what are you and Joe doing under that blanket? I thought you two were broken up?

Mary: We are; exes with benefits.

ex-door neighbor

The person who used to be but is no longer your next-door neighbor.

I invited my ex-door neighbor from California; I hope you don't mind.

execubabble

Verbal executive communication in broad, vague terms that rise above normal speak. Characterized by an excessive use of executive words such as "robust," "paradigm," and "drill down." Those on the receiving end of execubabble are no better informed after the speech than when it began.

Me: How is the company doing?

My boss: We are entering a quarter in which we expect robust growth. Paradigms are shifting, but the team has drilled down to the heart of the challenge.

ex-hole

Your asshole ex-husband, ex-boyfriend, or just plain ex. A person you used to be with but you can't stand now.

Yeah, my ex-hole wants to get back together, but there is no possible way.

expiration chug

Drinking milk very quickly on the day of the expiration date.

Josh: What happened to that gallon of milk in the refrigerator?

Greg: Oh, I gave it an expiration chug, so it wouldn't go bad.

Josh: Good thinking!

expiration dating

To start a relationship that has a defined end date (e.g., one of the people is moving soon).

Jay: I hear you started dating some new girl.

John: Yeah, but she's moving across the country in a month, so we're planning on breaking up.

Jay: A little expiration dating, eh?

extheist
Someone who was raised with religion but later abandoned the practice.

Courtney: Are you an atheist?

Brooks: Nah, but I was raised a Catholic. I stopped practicing years ago. I guess you could call me an extheist.

eye candy
Something purely aesthetically pleasing. Can be a person, a film, a sunset, a flower, or anything else you can see.

Nicole is oozing with hotness, and she's total eye candy to every man.

face base

The point in a romantic relationship when pictures of the couple begin to appear on Facebook, and/or when the relationship status changes to "In a relationship."

Holly: It looks like Kat has made it to face base with that new guy.

Donna: Yeah, his picture is all over her profile now.

Facebook crush

The unexplainable urge to revisit a Facebook friend's photos tab repeatedly, and checking to see if other friends have written new messages on their wall. Usually afflicts users who are only somewhat acquainted.

I've got a Facebook crush on a guy I was going to rent a room from, but in the end we just friended each other.

Facebook fever

The uncontrollable urge to check one's Facebook every time one comes in contact with a computer.

Sam: Dude, you've been on the computer for four hours reloading the same page. Don't you have a final exam tomorrow?

Kyle: Facebook fever.

Sam: No one has posted on your wall in days.

Kyle: How do you know? They could have posted in between now and the last time that I reloaded the page!

Facebook foreplay

Writing increasingly sexy messages back and forth on Facebook.

The Facebook foreplay was hot, but in person it just wasn't there.

Facebook surprise

When you don't know a picture has been taken of you until you see it uploaded by someone else on Facebook. Usually results in an embarrassing picture getting into the public's viewership, though it can be a normal, innocent picture.

I got wasted and started getting rowdy with this hogbeast, but I didn't think anyone saw and I got away with it. Unfortunately I got a Facebook surprise when I saw Jen uploaded pics from that party and it had some embarrassing photos.

Facebookable

Appropriate enough to be viewed by the general public of the Facebook community (i.e., friends/significant others/family/coworkers) without having to worry about explaining a sketchy situation.

You know it was a good night when only 3 out of 152 pics are Facebookable.

Facebrag

To use Facebook as a platform to brag, normally about a job, internship, trip, purchase, or anything else that nobody really needs to know but you'd like to tell everyone because you're awesome.

Sample Facebook status: Jane Stephens is headed to London with her new iPhone for her 2nd JOB INTERVIEW!!!!! :))))

Paul: Hey, did you see Jane's newest Facebrag? Eesh.

fake take

Pretending to enter and store someone's phone number into your mobile phone after they generously offer up their phone number and say, "Take my number and give me a call sometime."

Jeff: Why did you take that loser's number and tell him you'll call him?

Chris: Don't worry, dude, it was a fake take.

fall on the grenade

The noble act of being a wingman. A group of male buddies are at a bar flirting with a group of hotties. All of a sudden the hotties' ugly girlfriend comes out of the ladies' room. That's the grenade! It's the solemn duty of one of the men to fall on the grenade and hook up with that beastwoman so his friends can hook up with the hotties.

It's Peter's turn to fall on the grenade. I think we should all buy him a pity round first.

fallback program

The show that you watch while your main show is on a commercial. It is usually not as good as your main show.

Dude, I was watching Family Guy *last night and there was a twelve-minute commercial. Good thing I had* SpongeBob *as my fallback program.*

famine underwear

The garments you wear during a shortage of underwear, when you haven't done laundry in several weeks or months. Usually characterized by lack of elasticity, holes (usually large and awkwardly located), stains, and an age of at least five to ten years. In some cases soccer shorts, underwear of unknown origin, thongs, bathing suit bottoms, or granny panties can be considered famine underwear, even if they do not necessarily meet the above criteria.

I haven't done laundry in weeks, so I'm wearing my famine underwear—the boxers I made in home economics in middle school.

fanboy

A breed of human male who is obsessed with either a fictional character or an actor. Often follows various elements of geek culture (e.g., sci-fi, comics, *Star Wars*, video games, anime, hobbits, Magic: the Gathering, etc.) and lets his passion override social graces. Also see "fangirl."

At the mall, I almost got mowed over by some Dragon Ball Z *fanboy on his skateboard.*

fanfic

Short for "fan fiction." A story written by a fan of a particular art (movie, book, TV show, video game, etc.)

about the characters and world in that series, usually without the original creator's permission. Plural: "fanfics."

By the very nature of fanfic, there're a lot of really terrible fics out there. But it's great when you find a good one!

fangirl

A breed of human female who is obsessed with either a fictional character or an actor. Fangirls tend to congregate at anime conventions and on fan blogs. Have been known to emit high-pitched sounds, as well as glomp, grope, and tackle when encountering their particular obsessions. Often claim that "I'm really gonna marry him cuz we R ment 2 b!!!!!!!11111!!!!!!@#$347903458134! @!@!" Also uses excessive amounts of punctuation.

Hugh Jackman: 'Ello.

Fangirl: Squeeeeee! (Immediately attaches to Jackman's leg.)

Jackman: Security!

fantasy cheering

Rooting for a football player you would normally root against because the player is on your fantasy football team.

As the home team was losing, the crowd became frustrated with John's fantasy cheering for the opposing quarterback.

fappable

Something that is sexually desirable, or deemed high enough quality that it can be used for masturbation purposes. (From "fap," the onomatopoeic representation of masturbation.)

Man, that picture is really fappable.

fart enthusiast

An individual who is highly amused by anything associated with flatulence.

LuAnn is such a fart enthusiast that, upon the mention of a fart, she doubles over with laughter.

farticles

The particles of air contaminated after someone or something lets out gas.

I don't want to breathe your farticles!

farting gift

A fart left immediately before exiting a room, leaving that special something to be remembered by.

Drake: That party was the worst.

Tony: Don't worry, I made sure to thank them with a farting gift.

farting terms

A milestone in a new relationship when both parties feel at ease when breaking wind in front of each other.

You've been with that bird for a long time, and you're not even on farting terms yet? Do you have to go to the bathroom every time you need to rasp?

fashionably late

The refined art of being just late enough (five minutes or so) to give the impression that you are a busy, popular person who was held up with other business.

She arrived at the party fashionably late.

fat finger

To make a typo. Often used when referring to password typos.

You didn't get my email? I must have fat fingered the address.

fauxhawk

Like a mohawk, but instead of shaving the sides of your head, you just glue up the middle part in the style of a mohawk.

Ladies want me because I got a fauxhawk.

fauxlationship

A temporary relationship to relieve emptiness caused by the lack of a real relationship. Also used to describe relationships with no commitment. Not a very responsible idea.

I don't trust her, man. It looks like a fauxlationship to me.

fauxpology

When a person makes it sound like they are apologizing when, in fact, they are just shifting the blame or using twisted logic to argue their way out of responsibility for their actions.

When George said, "I guess we all just have to accept some of the blame here," I stopped listening, because I knew it was just going to be another fauxpology.

f-bomb

1. A euphemism for the f-word. (Also known as "effinheimer.")

DC was droppin' f-bombs all over, yo, until his grandma heard him and washed his mouth out.

2. A euphemism for the word "friend" when used in the breakup conversation. Usually only used by the dumpee.

Her: I think we should just be friends, Jim.

Him: Why you droppin' the f-bomb on me? That's cold.

feed the beast

To send a high-maintenance partner a text message in order to keep them sweet and avoid them getting upset that you are ignoring them. Similar to feeding a Tamagotchi. You send these texts to keep the relationship alive.

Colin: You coming to the pub, mate?

Guy: Yeah, of course. One minute, though—I just gotta feed the beast first.

femullet

The female version of the mullet. Commonly paired with cancer-spotted skin, way too much blue eyeshadow, Hooters shirts, and farm equipment.

That trashy lady's femullet looks like she got hit with her husband's sheepshearing blade.

finger guns

A way for creepy people with porn mustaches to say "hello" or "I understand." Hold your fingers in the shape of guns (use both hands for maximum effect) and point at someone who just arrived. Bend thumbs to simulate shooting your finger guns and make a clicking sound with your mouth. May be accompanied with a wink in extreme cases.

That dude who looks like he just fell out of the '70s offered me a piece of candy and then winked and gave me finger guns. I said no.

fire hazard

A man who is in denial of his homosexuality (in the closet) despite the fact that he is clearly gay to the objective observer.

Hey, Mike, Jessica's fire hazard of a husband was checking out your ass again.

five-second rule

An unwritten law dictating that if a food or other consumable item is dropped onto the floor, it may be picked up and eaten within five seconds. The reasoning behind this is that dirt and germs take six seconds to transfer from one surface to another.

Oops, dropped my Popsicle. Five-second rule! (Proceeds to pick up dirty-ass rocket pop and suck the lint off of it.)

flat tire

Stepping on the back of someone's shoe to make it come off or make them trip.

When I gave him a flat tire everyone laughed.

flavorgasm

Involuntary moan you let out when eating food that is so good. Usually happens on the first bite.

I ate this unbelievable steak yesterday. I swear I had a total flavorgasm.

flex

To make a statement, clearly express yourself, or threaten verbally, more than physically.

Oh, you wanna flex? Okay, step outside—I'll show you what's up! No? That's what I thought.

flip a bitch

To make an illegal U-turn, usually in the middle of a street or over a double line. Often results in passengers' freaking out.

Just flip a bitch here. There's no cops around.

flirtationship

When you regularly flirt with an acquaintance or friend but do no more.

Bob has only one girlfriend, but starts a flirtationship with almost every girl he meets.

flojectile

The bits of food matter that fly onto your mirror while you are flossing your teeth.

I need to wash those flojectiles off my bathroom mirror before the health department shuts me down.

fo' shizzle, my nizzle

Affirmative response. A bastardization of "fo' sheezy, mah neezy," which is a bastardization of "for sure, mah nigga," which is a bastardization of "I concur with you wholeheartedly, my African-American brother."

Kid 1: It's late. I'm heading back to the hizzouse. You stayin'?

Kid 2: Fo' shizzle, my nizzle.

FOMO

Fear of missing out.

Even though he was exhausted, John's FOMO got the best of him, and he went to the party.

food baby

When you eat so much your stomach looks pregnant.

Jeez! I ate so much—look at this food baby!

food coma

The feeling of listlessness, bordering on sleep, that one feels after eating a large meal, often caused by a rush of blood to the stomach and intestines during food digestion.

Man, we ate the whole pu pu platter, and now I'm slipping into a food coma.

food douche

A person who thinks they know the best place to get any one specific item of food and that the places you know all suck.

Jason: I love this turkey sandwich.

Joey: This sandwich sucks; I know a place with the best turkey sandwich I have ever had.

Jason: You are such a food douche.

foody call

A phone call, text, or conversation to a friend or friends for obtaining food with no prior planning.

Lisa made a foody call at 9:45 a.m. on Saturday, and by 10:30 we were sitting in The Original Pancake House chowing on pancakes and bacon.

foreploy

The act of misrepresenting yourself for the sole purpose of getting laid.

The whole evening was foreploy. The dickhead only wanted to hit it.

foul-weather friend

The opposite of a fair-weather friend, a foul-weather friend only seeks you out if they have a problem, need a shoulder to cry on, a ride to town, or someone to watch their dog, but otherwise they act as if they don't even know you. They're only your chum when they're glum.

As soon as I got a new job and a decent place to live, my foul-weather friend stopped speaking to me.

freeboobing

Not wearing a bra under a shirt. Analogous to freeballing for men, which means not wearing underwear.

Roxanne is not wearing a bra under her shirt. Therefore, she is freeboobing.

free-timer

Unlike a part-timer or a full-timer, a free-timer has no job, so they have a lot of free time.

Curt: So, what do you do during the week?

Girl in club: Oh, I'm a free-timer.

Freudian click

Sending an email to someone by mistake.

A second after I hit "send," I realized that I had made a Freudian click and emailed a love note to my ex instead of my boyfriend. So embarrassing!

friend custody

When a couple breaks up, one person gets to keep the mutual friends while the other must find new ones because being around each other would be too awkward. The person who keeps the friends is said to be granted friend custody.

Bob: Why don't you come out with us tonight?

Phil: Because when Jane and I broke up, she got friend custody.

friend high

The pleasant high feeling one feels around close friends, often compared to being on some sort of drug. Accompanied by lots of laughing, stupidity, excitement, good conversation, and loud obnoxiousness. Getting "high" off another's good friendship vibes. Often considered a replacement for drugs and alcohol, though not heavily supported.

Let's hotbox this room with our friend high!

friend zone

Where you end up after you fail to impress a woman you're attracted to. Often initiated by the woman saying, "You're such a good friend." Usually associated with long days of suffering, and watching your love interest hop from one bad relationship to another.

I spent all that money on a date, just to find out she put me in the friend zone. (Said with eerie echo . . .)

friendgirl

A woman with whom you are friendly but not in any way romantically linked.

My girlfriend is always jealous of Sandy, but Sandy's just my friendgirl. There's never been anything else going on between us.

frottage

To induce sexual pleasure by applying one's body to another's. The process is especially popular at music concerts and nightclubs. Also "dry humping."

I went to the club last night and was overwhelmed by all the frottage.

fuck-you tax

A nondiscretionary charge or fee placed on orders or purchases from certain companies, frequently ticket retailers and cinemas. The charge never relates to a specific cost incurred by the company and is purely an additional fee to boost profits. The company in question knows the consumer has no option but to pay, so their charging it is the company saying, "Fuck you, pay it."

A $3 "Booking Fee" on my movie tickets—that's just a fuck-you tax!

fugly

Combination of "funny" and "ugly" or "fucking" and "ugly."

She's so fugly no one will date her.

fularious

Combination of "funny" and "hilarious" or "fucking" and "hilarious."

That joke was fularious!

fully sick

Great. Of high quality.

Guy: Check out my fully sick ride!

Chick: Fully sick!

funky cold medina

A drink that drives ladies crazy and makes them want the man who buys it for them. After the title of a 1980s song by rapper Tone-Lōc.

Bartender, how about a funky cold medina for the lady?

G

1. A gangster.

That's a real G. Don't piss him off.

2. A thousand dollars.

Let me borrow a G.

3. A term of endearment.

What up, G?

gangsta lean

A common driving position in which the driver holds the wheel with his left hand while leaning to his right toward the passenger seat, usually bobbing his head or bumpin' with the beat. It's a pretty badass way to drive. This move works best in a Chevy Caprice or any pimp-style car with a three-person front seat.

Sammy was gangsta leanin' so hard yesterday that his head was partially out the passenger window. What a pimp.

gate rape

The TSA airport screening procedure.

My sister got gate raped at LAX.

gay buffer

When you sit down somewhere (usually in a movie theater) and purposely leave an extra seat between you and a person of the same sex so as not to appear gay.

Dude, leave me a gay buffer! You're so close to me you're practically sucking my dick.

gayby

The child of a gay couple.

Have you had the chance to see Dan and Terry's gayby? He is absolutely fabulous and cute as a button!

geek

Previously a four-letter word, now a six-figure salary.

Bill Gates is a geek, yet he is the richest man in the world.

geographobia

The irrational fear of traveling virtually anywhere due to fear of locational germs, illnesses, parasites, and dangers both real and exaggerated. Similar to agoraphobia in that sufferers limit the scope of their world, but more specific in that the nature of the perceived threat is directly related to any foreign location.

Magnus: So do you think Laurie will go on the camping trip?

Andy: No, she won't even leave Scranton, she's so geographobic.

ghetto bird

A police helicopter.

At least two ghetto birds were chasing Lorenzo down the I-10 last night after he jacked that car.

ghetto upgrade

When you are flying economy on a near empty flight and can lie across an entire row of seats.

I got a ghetto upgrade on my flight to Bangkok and was able to sleep most of the way.

ghost taste

The familiar taste that accompanies a postmeal burp. It's like déjà vu in your mouth.

Man, Jo, I just caught a straight ghost taste from that barbecue earlier.

gift crack

The gap in wrapping paper or uncovered portion of a gift usually found on the bottom of the box. May result from the gift wrapper running out of paper or cutting gift wrap too small to cover the entire package.

Bryan figured out what his present was because the gift crack exposed the picture on the box.

gift parasite

A person who adds their name to a gift tag in order to claim partial credit for giving the gift.

I'm totally broke, so I had to be a gift parasite and sign on that present you're giving Grandma.

girlfriend voice

The change in pitch or tone of a man's voice when talking to his significant other. The girlfriend voice is characterized by a higher pitch and a more effeminate tone with speech patterns scattered with pet names and childish words. This type of speech is usually frowned upon when used in the presence of other men and could result in a fair amount of ridicule.

Did you hear Bob's wicked girlfriend voice when he was talking to Lisa? Let's whip his ass!

girlfriend-proof

To hide any objects that you would rather your girlfriend not see. These objects usually include porn, childish things (dolls, small toys, etc.), and Pokémon memorabilia. You can girlfriend-proof your car, room, house, and really just about anything. Similar to parent-proofing.

Mitch: Hey, man, want to play me in a Yu-Gi-Oh! match?

Mike: Sorry, dude, I just got done girlfriend-proofing my room. All my cards are in a shoebox under my bed.

Mitch: Oh, all right. Hey, did you remember to take down your Justin Timberlake poster?

Mike: Oh, shoot. Thanks for reminding me. I'll get home and take care of that right away.

Gleeks

Fans of the TV show *Glee*.

We're such Gleeks, we've seen every episode twice.

glomp

To hug with enthusiasm. To pretty much tackle someone in greeting. When used online, often surrounded by "action stars"—asterisks denoting an action.

Girl A: *Glomps B* Welcome back! We missed you! How was your vacation?

Girl B: *Glomps A back* I missed you too! My vacation was great!

go primitive

Instead of keyboarding or texting a long and detailed story, using a phone call as a more direct way to have the conversation.

Dude, I'm good with texting but this is giving me carpal tunnel. Let's go primitive. I'll call you tomorrow at 8.

good looking out

To let someone know you are thankful for their watching out for you or helping you out with something.

Guy 1: Wut up, son? Seen yo' ex at da club just now.

Guy 2: Good lookin' out, whoadie. Let's hit a different place, fo' sho'.

good talk

A way to end a man-to-man conversation about personal feelings in a comfortable, heterosexual manner.

Marc: Dude, I think my girl is cheating on me. What should I do?

Scott: Dump that bitch.

Marc: Good talk.

Google harder

A phrase used in response to someone whining about not being able to find something on Google. An expert Googler would then show some semblance of pity and assist by immediately Googling for the information successfully.

Harrison: Dude, I don't know what it means to kill two frogs with one dart, and I can't freakin' find the definition on Google!

Jimmy: Google harder, you idiot. . . .

Googleganger

An individual with the same name as you whose records and/or stories are mixed in with your own when you Google yourself. Similar to a doppelganger.

Hey, I just Googled my name and found that I have three Googlegangers!

Googleheimer's

The condition where you think of something you want to Google, but by the time you get to your computer, you have forgotten what it was.

I've got Googleheimer's so bad that, between the garage and the office, I forgot what I was going to look up.

googly eyes

Occurs when a person sees someone they like a lot. It's the way they look at the person when they cannot find the words to express how they feel. The way someone looks at the person who has them sprung. It doesn't necessarily mean having big, huge eyes. Just staring a lot.

He's got me all googly eyes.

gotcha journalism

When the media entraps its subjects by asking simple, straightforward questions that cannot be answered by inept politicians.

Katie: Governor, how many fingers am I holding up?

Sarah: You know, Katie, I'm sick and tired of this gotcha journalism.

grade digger

Girl who only talks to you for help with her classes.

Kurt: Yo, who was that chick at the union?

McHale: Nothing, grade digger.

Grand Theft impairment

The four-hour period of time that you cannot drive or function in society after playing *Grand Theft Auto* because you may have the urge to steal a car, kill innocent people, and/or drive recklessly.

Caitlin: Hey, you wanna come pick me up so we can go to the movies?

George: Aww, I wish, but I have Grand Theft impairment. I can come later, though.

grip

1. An abundant amount of something.

Yo! I got a grip of cash today. Let's go spend it.

There's no need to buy more beer; I have a grip at home.

2. An undefined unit of time, usually to express a long period as opposed to a short period.

What up, man? I haven't seen you for a grip.

GTL

The process of staying fresh and mint. Stands for "gym, tan, laundry." Must be done every day to achieve maximum potential. Side effects include fist pumping. Coined by the eloquent Mike "The Situation" Sorrentino from MTV's groundbreaking *Jersey Shore*.

You gotta GTL every day to make sure you're looking your best, bro. If your shirt looks bad it makes the whole product look bad.

guilt floss

When one flosses one's teeth right before a dentist appointment so that, when asked if one flosses, one can answer "yes."

In hopes of making up for months of ignoring the hygiene of his teeth, John did a quick guilt floss before driving to the dentist.

guilt wave

The wave given by a driver who just cut in ahead of you in traffic or knowingly did something that was completely wrong on the road.

I was about to make a turn when this dude comes speeding by, almost hitting me. He stopped at the last second and gave me a guilt wave.

guitar face

The unusual face some people make while playing the guitar. Typically resembles a look of pain, intense ecstasy, or sometimes even plain old gas.

Man, that solo was sweet, but he had total guitar face going on.

gullible

The only word that is not in the dictionary.

I swear, gullible is not there.

ha

Acknowledgment of someone's comment or joke, indicating it wasn't funny.

John: I love girls who wear their PJs all day long. It's like they are ready to jump in bed at a moment's notice.

Jack: Ha.

hahaha

To express on AIM when something was funny, because just "haha" isn't that dramatic and can be used to just acknowledge when someone has said something.

Bobby31: . . . they call it cheese and quackers!

Annette85: haha

Bobby31: oh come on it was funnier than that

Annette85: hahaha

hand-me-up

When the young generation in a family adopts and purchases new technology at a fast rate, old versions (that are in working order but are not up to current standards) are given to the parents or older generations. Commonly occurs multiple times on commodity technology gadgets, leaving parents with many gadgets to play with.

I purchased a new computer to replace my "slow" computer, which I gave to my grandpa as a hand-me-up.

hangry

When you are so hungry that your lack of food causes you to become angry, frustrated, or both. An amalgam of "hungry" and "angry."

Damn! Where is that steak I ordered? We've been waiting for an hour and a half here. The service here is terrible! I'm starving! I don't know about you, but I'm starting to feel really hangry!

hasbian

A former lesbian who is now in a heterosexual relationship.

Mona is a hasbian. She used to date chicks, but now she wants to date men.

hater tots

Like haterade, the figurative snack you consume when you're hating on someone.

Remy: He acts like he's the shit because he has that Mercedes SLR.

Louis: Man, you need to cut down on all those hater tots you've been eating.

have a wide stance

To be a homosexual, especially one who is closeted. Coined from the transparent defense of Senator Larry Craig to charges of disorderly conduct stemming from his apparent solicitation of an undercover officer from underneath the partition of a restroom stall. Prior to pleading guilty, Senator Craig attempted to explain his behavior by claiming that his shoe touched the officer's underneath the partition because he had a wide stance when going to the bathroom.

Genevieve is really crushing hard on the varsity QB. Someone should tell her that the dude has a wide stance.

HBIC

Head bitch in charge.

I am the HBIC up in here. Bow down, bitches.

head splinter

A painfully annoying song that gets stuck in your head, in extreme cases, impeding everyday tasks.

I've got "I Don't Feel Like Dancin'" stuck in my head; it's a real head splinter!!

headphone syndrome

When someone is wearing headphones and speaks very loudly because he or she tries to speak over the music.

Mike: Hey, man, how's it going?

Joe: I'M FINE. WHAT'S UP WITH YOU?!!!!!

Mike: Whoa, man, watch it! You're suffering from a little bit of headphone syndrome.

heart-on

A warm feeling in one's heart. A feeling of awe, astonishment, surprise, or admiration.

The way Vicki Valerie sings gives me a major heart-on!

Heisman

1. In American football, when an offensive player pushes a defensive player away with one arm in order to flee and/or incapacitate the defensive player, emulating the pose on the Heisman Trophy.

Wow, did you see Ricky Williams Heisman that linebacker?

2. A direct and impersonal rejection of a sexual overture, pass, or advance.

She gave him the Heisman when he smiled at her over his martini.

3. A skillful dodging of an impending and usually negative engagement or interaction.

I Heismanned my boss yesterday when he approached me about those TPS cover sheets and reports.

hella

1. Very, totally.

2. Lots of. Short for "a hell of a lot of."

Guy 1: That party was hella sketch. What was with all those skanky-ass girls?

Guy 2: There was hella weed, tho!

heteroflexible

I'm straight—but shit happens.

Dude, it's not my fault. I was drunk and it was fun. What can I say? I'm heteroflexible.

hiberdating

Someone who ignores all their other friends when they are dating a boyfriend or girlfriend.

I haven't seen or heard from Jennifer since she started hiberdating Teddy four months ago.

high ten

A double-handed high five, reserved for especially awesome scenarios.

High five: Dude, you screwed the head cheerleader!

High ten: Dude, you screwed the entire cheerleading team!

highlighter abuser

A student who tends to highlight almost every part of an academic text he or she is reading, thus defeating the purpose of highlighting in the first place. Typically an attentive student, but can't grasp the actual significance of what he or she is reading.

Tim was ashamed to find Janie had indiscriminately highlighted virtually every sentence in her packet about Kafka. It all made so much sense now. She was a highlighter abuser.

highway salute

An extended middle finger from a fist thrust forth whilst driving, as a gesture of anger toward the person it is aimed at.

That prick is tailgating me. I think I'll give him the ol' highway salute.

himbo

The male version of a bimbo, whore, or slut.

He's such a himbo that he'd sleep with anything that has, or had, a pulse.

hit the slide

To quit one's job in a truly stunning fashion.

Steven was fed up with working for assholes, so he hit the slide.

hobosexual

The opposite of metrosexual; one who cares little for one's appearance.

Peter Jackson makes great movies, but he's a hobosexual.

holidaze

The feelings of confusion and excitement people have between Thanksgiving and Christmas; the blur one feels after/during shopping for gifts in crowded retail stores with heavy holiday traffic.

Finley sat on the couch in a holidaze after a day of hectic Christmas shopping on Black Friday.

home skillet

Friend.

Word up, my home skillet.

homing from work

Using work time and resources for personal tasks. The opposite of telecommuting.

Busey: Steve, did you download those episodes of Entourage *I told you about?*

Myers: I told you, Gary, my home Internet connection sucks ass. I am going to download and burn them while I am homing from work.

homoblivious

Lacking gaydar.

He was so homoblivious that he didn't know that guy was coming on to him.

hostage lunch

Meal (often pizza) purchased by the company and delivered for employees whose bosses require them to attend a meeting or work during their lunch hour.

I was planning on running some errands over my lunch hour, but the VP is keeping us in a meeting. At least he ordered us hostage lunch.

hotness hypnosis

Trancelike state you enter when you find someone so physically attractive that you overlook serious personality flaws.

Brad finally woke from hotness hypnosis and started to realize that Angelina was batshit crazy.

hugh wear

An extensive wardrobe of bathrobes.

Duder 1: Hey, man, nice closet. What's with all the robes?

Duder 2: You know I like to be comfortable AND stylin' 24/7.

Duder 1: Wow, you have a complete line of hugh wear up in here. Now all you need are some skeezy blondes.

Hulk out

To become enraged; to lose one's temper, clothing, and power of coherent speech before embarking on a spree of violence and wanton destruction. After the comic book character who turned from an unregarded geek into a thundering green mass of unstoppable fury.

It all happened so fast . . . the Broncos ran in their fifth touchdown and he just Hulked out. I hope he's going to pay for a new TV. And window.

hump day

The middle of a workweek (i.e., Wednesday). Often referred to in the context of climbing a proverbial hill to get through a tough week.

Thank god it's hump day—the weekend starts in two days!

hype aversion

Rejection of an insanely popular idea, game, show, place, etc., simply because it is so insanely popular.

April: I'm enjoying season three of Lost.

Laura: Season three came out four or five years ago.

April: I know, I suffer from hype aversion.

hyphy

Stupid, silly, drunk, high, and just generally out of hand.

We got hyphy in da parking lot after the club let out!

I

I know, right?

An affirmation that you agree with or can relate to the preceding statement. It can be used whether the speaker actually knows or not, but it usually means that the speaker can identify with the preceding statement.

Selena: I got so drunk at the party that I puked when I got home.

Maya: I know, right? I think I might have barfed up stuff from last year.

iCamp

To participate in the long line that forms overnight outside of Apple retail stores for new products. An iCamper will have all his supplies to make it through the night, such as a tent, flashlight, sleeping bag, urine bottle, gun, etc. Often happens at Apple stores in large cities.

Jim: Hey, did you get the new iPad?

Howard: Yeah, I had to iCamp at the Apple store on Fifth all night long to get it.

ice maker

The opposite of an icebreaker. Something you do when meeting someone that makes it super awkward.

Dan: Hey, you're in my Spanish class, right? I'm Dan.

Christine: Oh yeah, I'm Christine. We should totally hang out sometime.

Tony (butting in with an ice maker): Dude, DAN, we gotta go over to my place. We're gonna have a huge orgy with these Brazilian quadruplets.

Dan: Uh . . .

ignoranus

A person who is not only ignorant, but is also an asshole.

Mike is such a snobby know-it-all. I wish he wasn't such an ignoranus all the time.

I'm good

Rejection of, and often ridicule for, an offered good or service by feigning satiation when "No, thank you" just won't do.

Ray-Ray: Do you want to go down to the Creepy Crawl and see The Wheezing Coughers?

Jess: No, thanks, I'm good.

I'm gonna let you go

Phrase that means "I want to get off the phone now because I hate talking to you, but I'll pretend that I'm being polite by letting you go back to whatever boring crap you would be doing if you weren't talking to me."

Them: So then he said it was benign but I should probably get it removed. And I said—

You: Wow! That's nuts! Hey look, I'm sure you've got a lot of stuff to take care of. I'm gonna let you go. Bye.

Them: Oh, uh, yeah. Bye.

I'm just sayin'

Something you say when someone is offended by something you just said. It removes all the offensiveness of the previous statement, making it all good.

Ryan: That chick has nice tits!

Rob: Damn, that's my sister!

Ryan: I'm just sayin'.

Rob: Oh, okay, it's cool.

I'm out of practice

An explanation for why you can't do something that requires being in shape. You're pretty much saying that you're out of shape—you're just not saying you're fat.

Jimmy: I'll race you!

Nate: Nah, I'm out of practice!

Jimmy: Fat ass.

immaculate congestion

When traffic is backed up for miles on a highway, crawling along—and then suddenly everyone returns to normal high speeds without passing an accident, stalled car, or road construction.

We spent forty-five minutes bumper to bumper for no reason?! It must be immaculate congestion.

immaturation

The process of becoming immature.

By revisiting old posts we were able to witness the immaturation of the Internet from a place of cordial dissent to a place of whiny bickering.

inbox rot

What happens when you neither accept nor decline a friend request from someone on Facebook or Myspace. Occurs in situations when you don't want to friend that person, but you also don't want to be rude by declining.

Dude, that asshole friend of my girlfriend just sent me a friend request on Facebook. He's getting the inbox rot.

indie

An obscure form of rock you only learn about from someone slightly more hip than yourself.

The indie kid introduced me to Modest Mouse, Built to Spill, and Rilo Kiley.

indoorsman

A person who spends considerable time in indoor pursuits, such as computing, sleeping, and watching sports on TV.

Sean, an avid indoorsman, is highly regarded for his skill at video games and computer programming.

interesting

Word used to describe something that arouses no interest at all. Used to politely avoid admitting indifference.

Wow, your bottle cap collection is . . . interesting.

internest

The cocoon of blankets, pillows, duvets, and other comfy things you gather around yourself to keep warm while spending long amounts of time on the Internet.

Tom knew that eating pizza in his internest was a bad idea, but it was just too warm and snuggly.

Internet

A vast array of pornography and advertisements.

I took the initiative in creating the Internet.

Internet coma

When you are sitting on your couch, feet up on the coffee table, laptop on your lap, and four to ten hours later you are in an entirely prone position with your legs off the edge of the coffee table and your head on the seat cushion, completely unresponsive to your surroundings. Symptoms include loss of peripheral vision, amnesia, severely reduced motor function ability, and drooling with one eye closed.

I got online this morning to check my email and mess around on Facebook for a bit. Next thing I know it's 7 p.m., my legs are totally numb, and I have this nasty trail of dried drool down my chin. That Internet coma completely ruined my day!

Interweb

A sarcastic term for the Internet. Often used in the context of parody regarding an inexperienced, unskilled, or incoherent user.

Hey, guys, I'm using the Interweb!

intexticated

Word used to describe someone who is driving and texting.

Emily: How did she get in a car accident?

Lola: She was intexticated.

involuntary "you too"

The "you too" that automatically comes out of your mouth out of habit, even though it doesn't fit the moment. It happens to the best of us.

Girl: Well, happy birthday, man. Have fun at SeaWorld tomorrow.

Guy: Thanks, you too.

iPhone effect

After one person in the group brings out their iPhone, the rest follow suit, ultimately ending all conversation and eye contact.

Dave: Hey, what do you want to order for drinks?

Rich: Not sure, let's see what Imbibe *magazine has for their best beer this month.*

(First iPhone comes out of the pocket—enter Safari search.)

(Next iPhone comes out—enter Facebook post.)

(Third iPhone makes an entrance, and the iPhone effect has arrived.)

IRS

Income removal system.

The IRS folks tried to jack five grand off my bank account.

it is what it is

Phrase used often in the business world that can be translated as "fuck it."

The client changed the deadline to today? Well, it is what it is. . . .

it was in the news feed

An excuse you can use after getting caught Facebook creeping. It always works, though the suspicious individual will likely remain skeptical.

Sarah: Are you creeping on me? How did you know I commented on that picture?

Derek: No, it was in the news feed!

it's complicated

Refers to an ambiguous state between "friends" and "in a relationship." May also be used to indicate dissatisfaction with an existing relationship. After one of the options for "Relationship Status" on Facebook.

If someone changes their status from "In a Relationship" to "It's Complicated," expect them to be "Single" and "Looking for Random Play" soon.

J

jackass of all trades

A person who is exceptionally bad at everything.

Stefan is a dork. Give him anything to do and he'll screw it up. He's a jackass of all trades.

jawn

Thing. Item. Object.

Yo, hand me that jawn right there.

Jeebus

Jeebus was born more than 2,000 years ago, and started the religion of Crustianity. Jeebus Crust is the son of Gosh and part of the Holy 3-Some (or Ménage à Trois). Jeebus was born to Bloody Mary, a virgin, by a miracle of the Spirit of Truthiness. The Holy Babble gives an account of an angel visiting Bloody Mary to tell her that she was chosen to bear the Son of Gosh.

Jeebus Crust is the savior of the one and only true religion, Crustianity.

Jesus jeans

Ripped or "hol(e)y" jeans.

Dude! LOOK AT MY NEW JESUS JEANS!

JFGI

Acronym for "just fucking Google it." Said when somebody asks a stupid question for which they could just look up the answer.

Dude 1: Hey, dude, what does "entropy" mean?

Dude 2: JFGI, byatch!

jill off

The female version of jack off.

Her boyfriend was out of town, so she got in the hot tub to jill off.

jingle bowels

Gastrointestinal woes following a night of holiday overindulgence.

Someone spiked the eggnog and Justin spent copious porcelain time after waking up with a wicked case of the jingle bowels.

job talker

Someone who only talks about (and has nothing better to do than talk about) their job. They usually chronically complain about work.

I tried to hang out with Jim from accounting last week, but the guy is a total job talker. All he did was talk about work for two hours.

joke insurance

When two friends have a mutual understanding to laugh at each other's jokes, no matter how lame or awkward, thus lessening the social failure of the bad jokes.

I was talking to some girls the other day when I cracked a "yo momma" joke. Luckily, I had joke insurance with Chris, so I still ended up getting both their numbers. All Chris got was a weird look for his over-the-top laugh.

joke poach

When a joke is said quietly to a friend and that friend repeats it loud enough for the entire room to laugh.

Teacher: Belgium is the cockpit of Europe, and I'm not talking about airplanes.

Student 1 (to Student 2): I don't think anyone was thinking about planes!

Student 2: Haha! I don't think anyone was thinking about planes!

Class: AHAHAHAHAHA!

Student 1: Dude, total joke poach.

kick rocks

Rude expression used to tell someone to leave. Derived from the lonely gesture of kicking rocks when one is bored or depressed.

You said what?! Kick rocks before I stomp yo' punk ass!

kill two pigs with one bird

A modern version of "kill two birds with one stone." From the popular video game Angry Birds.

I was killing two pigs with one bird by eating lunch and playing Angry Birds at the same time.

kipe/kype

To steal, pilfer, or swipe something of small value, like a candy bar or some other commonly shoplifted item.

Jesse kiped some Pabst from the store while we distracted the clerk.

kitchenheimer's

Disease you have when you find yourself in the kitchen going around in circles because you can't remember what you were doing there. Usually happens in the morning, before you're fully awake.

I was in the kitchen this morning wondering what the hell I was looking for when the microwave beeped to remind me I was heating up my cup of coffee. My kitchenheimer's is getting worse!

knob

A complete moron. Synonym for "tool."

Dude, you're such a friggin' knob!

Kodak courage

An extra dose of courage and the tendency to go beyond one's usual physical limits when being filmed or photographed.

I was a bit nervous being the first to hit the jump, but when you're with the film crew you get that Kodak courage.

kthxbai

Message that means "I understand, but with much regret and much haste, I must be departing from our conversation."

newb2342: da partiez @ 4, b there!!1

lolz3r: kthxbai!!!!11

laborhood

The neighborhood in which you work, if different from the neighborhood in which you live.

Nah, I don't wanna hang out in SoHo tonight. I try to avoid my laborhood on weekends.

land it in the Hudson

An expression used to encourage yourself or someone else when it appears an endeavor is headed for a disastrous outcome (due mostly to external conditions). Based on when Captain "Sully" Sullenberger averted tragedy by successfully landing US Airways Flight 1549 in the Hudson River. Also, "land it like Sully."

The company is on the brink of failure, so let's land it in the Hudson.

last texter

Friend who always sends you a meaningless text after the obvious end of a text conversation, just to get the last text. They do this while totally oblivious to their uncontrollable habit.

OMG, Jan is SUCH a last texter it drives me crazy. The other day, she sent me a text "K" back after I texted her "don't text me, in a meeting." I had to dig out my phone again to clear it so it wouldn't keep vibrating for the rest of the meeting!

laundry limbo

Intentionally rewashing clothing simply because you don't feel like putting it away.

I had a shirt I knew was clean, but I was too lazy to hang it up, so I just kept it in laundry limbo.

Lego hair

A particularly shitty male haircut in which the sides cover the ears and the hair appears to be "snap on."

Cha Chi hadn't had a haircut in weeks, and when he showed up he had Lego hair.

less than three

Love. Refers to the common text icon "<3," which looks like a heart when rotated counterclockwise.

Goodbye, my less than three.

life password

The password that you use for every website, email account, Facebook, Twitter, everything. Having a life password is not a good idea, but everyone does it.

My friend found out my life password and wrecked my Facebook account, stole all my PayPal money, and emailed offensive images to my mother.

liptease

The act of putting on lipstick suggestively. The oral equivalent of a striptease.

Diane was giving me a liptease from across the room, so I went over and asked her out.

locationship

A brief romantic encounter usually occurring while traveling or on vacation, occasionally outwardly resembling a conventional relationship, but without any underlying commitment. May be rekindled at future opportunities.

Melissa? Yeah, she's cool. We had a brief locationship at the company retreat last fall.

lockblock

When one person prematurely tries to open the passenger door on a vehicle while the driver simultaneously tries to unlock the door, causing it to relock and keep the passenger outside.

Ty: Hey, man! Let me in the car already—it's cold out here!

Jovie: I've been trying to, but you've lockblocked me five times in a row now!

lol theory

The theory that the Internet phrase "lol," meaning "laugh out loud," can be placed at any part in any sentence and make said sentence lose all credibility and seriousness.

Doc: We need to operate on your colon, lol, you have cancer.

Jesus: Take this all of you and eat it, for it is my body, lol.

Me: Will you marry me? Lol.

love

Nature's way of tricking people into reproducing.

love tap

The gentle nudge of the car behind or in front of you that occurs in the process of parallel parking.

Oh man, this is a tight spot. I might have to love tap these cars a few times.

LQTM

Acronym for "laugh/laughing quietly to myself," which is a more accurate representation of the human response to funny things seen on the interweb than "LOL."

Boner jokes cause me to LQTM.

lying in wake

When a spouse or partner pretends to be asleep when you get home after a late night out, so they know what time you returned and can tear you a new one in the morning.

I tried to slip into bed last night without Megan noticing, but it turns out she was lying in wake. She gave me hell this morning.

M

madam's apple
A large bulge on a woman's trachea, possibly the sign of a male-to-female transvestite or transsexual, or it may simply be the luck of genetics.

Holy crap! Look at that madam's apple on Ann Coulter!

main
A person's number-one girl or guy, as opposed to the other partners they may have.

Yeah, man, I can't let my main find out about her because it's going to be a lot of trouble if she does!

maintenance texts
Sending text messages to people you'd like to eventually date to remind them that you exist. A low-effort way to maintain a connection without having to commit to anything serious.

Erin: Have you heard from that guy you met last week at the bar?

Jillian: Yeah, he sent me a few maintenance texts tonight, asking where we were but not wanting to meet up. LAME!

make it rain

When you're in a strip club with a stack, and you throw the money up in the air at the strippers so it seems to be raining money.

After Leroy finished trapping for the night, he went to the strip club, got ten stacks, and made it rain the whole night.

mall hangover

The headache, fatigue, and nausea you get after going to the mall.

I was at the mall for like five hours, and when I got home I had a major mall hangover.

man cave

A room, space, corner, or area of a dwelling that is specifically reserved for a male person to be in solitude, away from the rest of the household in order to work, play, or involve himself in certain hobbies or activities without interruption. This area is usually decorated by the male, without interference from female influence.

Tom retreated to his man cave to play his online RPG.

man chair

A chair in a women's clothes store/department for a guy to sit in and wait while his wife or girlfriend shops.

You go ahead and shop. I'll just be over here in the man chair.

man flu

The condition shared by all males wherein a common illness (usually a mild cold) is presented by the patient as life threatening. This is also known as "fishing for sympathy" or "chronic exaggeration." When the patient is your boyfriend, he will exhibit the standard symptoms (such as an overwhelming desire for compassion) while simultaneously rejecting any and all efforts you make to placate him.

You: Awww, you poor fella.

Him: I'm DYING!

You (soothingly): Oh, you're not dying.

Him (indignant): I AM! I have man flu!

You: Do you need some sympathy?

Him: Yes! But no one understands my pain. . . .

You: I understa—

Him: NO, YOU DO NOT!!

manicorn

A mythical male creature who is successful (pursues his passion and can pay his bills), funny, chivalrous, masculine, adventurous, and artistic (but not suicidal).

Too bad I settled when I got married. I just met my manicorn.

mansplain

To delight in condescending, inaccurate explanations delivered with rock-solid confidence of rightness and slimy certainty—because of course the speaker is right; he's the man in this conversation.

Even though he knew she had an advanced degree in neuroscience, he felt the need to mansplain that "there are molecules in the brain called neurotransmitters."

manther

An older man who preys on younger women. The male version of a cougar.

Mr. Smith is such a manther. Did you see his new girlfriend? She's got to be less than a quarter of his age.

mantrum

When a grown man throws a tantrum because he can't have his way.

Rick had a mantrum when he found out he couldn't have McDonald's for dinner.

marathoning

Watching an entire season of a TV series in a short period of time, especially in one sitting.

Hey, I can't come out tonight. I just got the last season of Lost, *and I'm marathoning it right now. I can't put it down.*

mascary

An overabundance of mascara.

Although Melanie thought her mascara application was flawless, her mascary really looked like creepy spider legs.

masturdating

Going out alone, like to a movie or a restaurant.

I saw No Country for Old Men *twice by myself. I'm addicted to chronic masturdating.*

mattress worship

When you stay in bed because you are too tired to get up and go to church.

I haven't been going to mass. I prefer mattress worship.

maybe later

A slightly less dick way of saying "no fucking way."

Kris: Hey, man, wanna come over later and catch Dancing with the Stars?

Dillon: Maybe later.

Kris: You fuckin' dick.

MBAese

The indecipherable language taught in MBA factories, where people have mastered the art of using large, multisyllabic words to make meaningless statements they think sound intelligent.

When the presenter says, "We are aggressively leveraging existing assets to affect a paradigm shift in interdepartmental synergy," the MBAese can be translated as, "We got a loan to buy a new phone, and then called Steve from HR."

M

meat sweats

Profuse sweating that results from consuming an obscene amount of meat.

I went to the Brazilian barbecue restaurant—the one with 30 different types of meat—and got the meat sweats!

meatspace

The real, flesh-and-blood world. As opposed to "cyberspace."

I met a great girl online, and I'm flying to Idaho to see her in meatspace.

mental masturbation

Intellectual activity that serves no practical purpose.

We debated and created a perfect system of government, but it was all just mental masturbation, really.

mental virginity

The general state of mind characterized by complete ignorance about sex and human reproduction.

Jaymie: Dude, they think that sex ed teaches us a heck of a lot of stuff we didn't know, but the truth is we lost our mental virginity awhile back.

Tucker: Totally, dude.

(high five)

merry textmas

The use of text messaging to send Christmas greetings.

Bob: Hey Sherry, who is blowing up your phone over there?

Sherry: Everyone is sending me merry textmases.

message anxiety

When you pause, freeze up, dread, or avoid the viewing of an email, text message, or voice mail that you fear might be bad or of major importance for you.

Hey, Mike, I just got an email from that girl I met last night. I have message anxiety about it—will you read it for me?

meta

Something that is characteristically self-referential.

Travis: So I just saw this film about these people making a movie, and the movie they were making was about the film industry. . . .

Tyler: Dude, that's so meta. Stop before my brain explodes.

meter-high club

In the spirit of the mile-high club, a club for those who couldn't afford plane tickets, so are just taking the train.

My girlfriend and I went for the meter-high club, but forgot that they can throw you off a train a lot easier than a plane.

metric shitload

A metric shitload is roughly 2.287 American measurement shitloads.

I've got a metric shitload of stuff to get done this weekend.

microwave mentality

The attitude that if something can't be done in five minutes or less, it's not worth doing.

Mom: You know, I just hate how our son never gets his chores done.

Dad: Yeah, it's his microwave mentality. He gets it from you.

midday crisis

The desperate need for a siesta because you're tired in the afternoon and coffee isn't cutting it any longer.

Working sucked today after that wild night of drinking. I had the worst midday crisis ever.

mimbo

Male version of a bimbo. Made famous by an episode of the sitcom *Seinfeld*.

My girlfriend left me for that mimbo who drives the ice cream truck.

mind over bladder

The power to be able to suppress any urination needs regardless of the urgency and pain it may cause.

Joe: Dude! Stop the car! I REALLY need to take a piss right now!!

Pete: No can do, man! Just use your mind over bladder!

MIRF

Acronym for "mom I'd run from." The opposite of a MILF. A mom you definitely would not want to do.

I don't know where she gets her good looks. Her mom is a MIRF!

missing link

A man who is covered head to toe with thick and wiry hair. He's so hairy, he's the missing link that connects humans to apes.

Joe: Damn, it's 115 degrees out here. Why doesn't Tom take off his shirt?

Dick: That poor bastard is so hairy, he got tired of being called the missing link.

mistext

A text message containing information (usually unflattering or damaging) about a third party that is sent to the individual it concerns rather than the person for whom the communication is intended.

Mistext written for secret lover is inadvertently sent to partner: On my way home, Elin suspicious, don't call.

mis-wave

To return a wave to someone you think is waving at you but is actually waving to the person behind you. Usually results in embarrassment and introversion.

Why was that person waving to me like he knew me? It must have been a mis-wave.

moneymoon

The time after your purchase of a good or service and before buyer's remorse happens.

The moneymoon is over. I realize now that buying that boat was a waste of money.

M

monthiversary

Like an anniversary, but occurs every month. For people who are overzealous about a new relationship.

Cara and Sloopy's monthiversary is January 5, 2012.

moobs

A combination of the words "man" and "boobs." This is what happens when fat gathers in a guy's chest area and gives him the appearance of having breasts. Usually seen in overweight males, but can also occur in men who are not really overweight.

Tommy: Those moobs are quite sizable.

Deron: Indeed.

mouse arrest

Getting grounded from the family computer.

Your mom after discovering your pornfolio: That's it. You are under mouse arrest, mister!

mouse potato

Someone who spends all their time on the computer surfing the net or playing games. Similar to a couch potato.

You spent seven hours on the Internet creating meanings for words on Urban Dictionary? Wow, you're such a mouse potato.

mow the laundry

Doing a load of laundry after allowing clothes to pile up on your bedroom floor for weeks.

Say, Maggie, suppose it's time to mow the laundry? I can't get your door open.

mutually assured distraction

The practice of distracting others in a manner that assures that neither party gets any work done.

We were both working on our papers, but then she started chatting with me on Facebook, and it was mutually assured distraction after that.

my phone's about to die

An expression commonly used to signal to another party that either a) you no longer want to text them, or b) you intend to hang up. This is a smooth way to avoid answering or hearing things from other people. Sometimes it's true, and your phone really is about to die, but that is rare.

Katie (speaking on the phone): So I've really been thinking about you a lot. I think I might love y—

Michael: Oh, shit, sorry, my phone's about to die! (click)

Chelsea (texting): My friend Kyle said he really digs u. what did u think about him?

Sam: sry my phones about 2 die

M

myspy

When you use Myspace to spy on ex-boyfriends, ex-girlfriends, ex-friends, or even your ex-boyfriend's ex-girlfriend's ex-boyfriend's baby mama.

My boyfriend caught me myspying on my ex-boyfriend's ex-girlfriend. Busted.

myth-information

Widely held and promoted but false information that has taken on a mythic quality. Misinformation.

September 11 conspiracy theories are based on myth-information.

nagotiate

Negotiation by attrition. When a friend, girlfriend, wife, etc., nags until she gets what she wants. (Or boyfriend, husband, etc.)

I wanted to stay home last night, but my wife nagotiated her way into going out to dinner.

name ambush

When an acquaintance you haven't seen for a long time greets you by name but you don't have time to remember their name.

Joe: Hi, Andy. How have you been?

Andy: Er . . . Hi. Good. How about YOU?

Sarah: Andy, you've just been name ambushed.

nano nap

An unintentional, seconds-long nap that you take most often in class or a really boring meeting. So short that usually nobody but you notices.

I caught myself taking a nano nap on that conference call.

natch

Abbreviation for naturally.

I am a member. So I went to the meeting, natch.

narsty

Combination of "gnarly" and "nasty." Something nasty that's actually kind of cool or strange. Also spelled "gnarsty."

That gal over there with the 5 o'clock shadow sure is narsty.

near-deaf experience

When you are listening to music on an MP3 player and a song that comes up is way louder than the previous one.

Well, Ke$ha is a lot louder than Passion Pit. I just had a near-deaf experience.

nearsighted date

As opposed to a blind date, where you have no idea what the other person looks like, a nearsighted date is one where you've seen a photo or chatted via webcam before meeting in person. This can often lead to disappointment if one person or the other has supplied misleading documentation.

That's the last nearsighted date I ever go on . . . her profile pic must have been five years, three hair colors, and two kids ago.

neighbornet

What you get when you connect to your neighbor's wireless Internet, with or without their knowledge.

Didja hear? Johnny connected his laptop to his neighbor's wireless network, and now he's got free neighbornet!

nerd

A person who is intensely interested in a particular hobby or topic. A geek with self-confidence. One whose IQ exceeds his weight.

Rich is quite a computer nerd.

nerd person

N

The voice someone uses when explaining something technical or generally nerdy.

I always switch to the nerd person when discussing the finer points of Ewok economics.

net lag

A feeling like jet lag that happens after you use your computer after sunset and the bright backlight tricks your body into thinking it's still daytime.

I was online until 3 a.m. last night, and now I feel like I'm still on Tokyo time. Net lag sucks.

netglow

Someone or something that is better online than in real life.

I've met him in real life. He is really below average without the netglow.

new year's block

A condition that usually takes place the first couple of weeks into the new year, in which a person keeps writing in the previous year in place of the new one.

Nadia: Doggone it! This is my third check today I wrote for 2011!

Karen: You're not alone! I got new year's block, too.

NFI

Acronym for no fucking idea.

The manager has NFI of the work that goes on around here.

nice

Word used as a filler during a pause in conversation. Doesn't necessarily mean something is good or nice.

Joel: I bought that new Fanta today.

George: Nice.

nillionaire

Person without any money of their own.

He looks rich, but it's all borrowed, and his bank account is nil; he's a nillionaire.

niteflix

Dreams so complex in plot and rich in production value that they seem like feature-length films.

Wow! I had niteflix last night. The only things missing were the end credits. I wonder if Steven Spielberg has niteflix, too.

no hair off my balls

Phrase that means "I don't care, won't harm me a bit, won't stress over it."

We can go in your car if you want. No hair off my balls.

no homo

Something you say to show that you aren't gay after saying something that sounds gay.

His ass is mine. No homo.

no offense

A phrase used to make insults seem socially acceptable.

No offense, John, but your mom is a fucking whore.

You've got huge bitch tits, Patrick . . . no offense.

no stalk

Phrase used before one inadvertently says something that sounds stalkerish on Facebook.

Carter: No stalk, but I noticed you changed your quotes on your profile. I love Hunter S. Thompson too!

Jane: Okaaay.

nod of acknowledgement

A standard among guys as a way to let the person know that you see them, without having to resort to using words. Girls will generally not accept the nod of acknowledgement and will instead opt for a wave of the hand and/or a smile, perhaps even accompanied by words. The nod of acknowledgement is a wordless conversation. The only acceptable response to a nod of acknowledgement is another nod. If you speak, you have broken the point of such a gesture.

Situations in which the nod of acknowledgement may be used:

Walking past a friend to class.

Catching a friend's eye across the room to say "hi."

Giving approval of a friend's actions.

nom nom nom

The sound made when someone is eating or chewing something and really enjoying it.

Chuck: Hey, are you eating my brownies?

Larry: Nom nom nom.

nomonym

When you eat something and it tastes like something else. For example, things often taste like chicken.

Neal: This tuna tastes just like your mom.

Micah: Dude, that's a nomonym!

no-motion

A promotion without a raise or bonus. In times of recession, employers try to give promotions to employees (e.g., adding more responsibility to their current position and/or a new job title) but not giving the employee any monetary compensation for it (e.g., no raise, no bonus).

My boss gave me a no-motion. I'm a VP now, but I still make the same pay as before!

no-name basis

Becoming so comfortable with someone that you no longer even use their first name.

Man: Honey, I'm home!

Woman: Hey, Baby, how was your day?

Man: It was great, Sweetheart.

Woman: What's my name?

Man: Ummmmmmmmm . . . Sweetheart?

Woman: What, are we on a no-name basis now?

nonversation

A completely worthless conversation, wherein nothing is illuminated, explained, or otherwise elaborated upon. Typically occurs at parties, bars, or other events where meaningful conversation is nearly impossible.

Smith: What a waste of time it is talking to that guy.

Jones: I know, every time I do, it's like a complete nonversation.

noted

A reply posted when someone puts a status on Facebook, Myspace, etc. Sarcastically shows that you care, and are going to write the status down in a notebook, when you really don't care at all.

Facebook status: John Smith is goin to the movies.

Comment: Noted.

nowhere story

A tale or recount of an event or events that doesn't ever reach a particular point or meaning.

Duder 1: So the other day I went into Foot Locker and saw a girl working there, so I thought it was Lady Foot Locker, but it turns out it wasn't.

Duder 2: Wow, dude, thanks for that nowhere story.

NSFL

Acronym for "not safe for life." Goes a step beyond NSFW (not safe for work), because it doesn't matter where you view the material—you will be scarred.

Why did I click on "Goatse"? That shit is NSFL.

Obama baby

A child conceived by way of celebratory sex after Obama was proclaimed president, or any baby born while Barack Obama's in office.

I was born July 2009. I'm an Obama baby!

objectively attractive

A descriptor used by a spouse or significant other who is incapable of admitting they find another person truly handsome, beautiful, or sexually attractive.

Well, I guess that guy over there is objectively attractive, but I don't find him interesting.

obsessive computer disorder

Disorder someone has when they are constantly online, or just on a computer, for fun or entertainment, and/or always thinking about anything computer related.

My father, who has obsessive computer disorder, a.k.a. OCD, lives on the computer and rarely leaves his room.

o'dark hundred

The hours before the sun comes up. A play on military time.

Oh shit, I gotta wake up at o'dark hundred tomorrow morning.

off the hook

Describes something so cool and in demand that it's busy all the time, like a phone that's always occupied. Out of control.

Man, that cat was fighting six people, and he beat them all. It was off the hook—you should have seen it!

office hands

Soft hands from doing office work and little or no hard labor.

He has office hands from his job.

He has soft office hands.

office quarterback

A manager infamously known for handing off their work and other useless assignments to you that they could and should be doing themselves.

The office quarterback just handed off a bunch of TPS reports to me, AGAIN!

oh-shit handle

The handle in most vehicles located in the interior of the vehicle above the door. Used in extreme driving situations where passengers do not wish to be thrown around the interior of the vehicle. Situations that warrant the usage of the "oh-shit handle" include hard braking, abrupt cornering, skidding, and careening off a bridge.

Me: Mike, I'm going to take the 25 mph turn at 55. Better grab the oh-shit handle!

Mike: I've been holding the oh-shit handle since you started the car!

one-cheek bench sneak

The easing out of flatulence gently, usually when sitting down, so as not to attract undue attention.

I was on a date, so I had to pull the one-cheek bench sneak.

one-upper

An annoying person who responds to hearing someone else's experience or problem by immediately telling a similar story about themselves with a much more fantastic (or terrible) outcome.

Person: I have a dislocated knee.

One-upper: Yeah, well, last summer, I broke my leg in four places, and had to have a steel pin inserted. I also had to have surgery done on my knee to repair the torn ligaments. I was on crutches for almost two months.

one-yard stare

Similar to the 1,000-yard stare that veterans acquire, a trait that people who work in cubicles or open workspaces pick up as they learn to ignore or avoid noticing anything that is not on their computer monitor.

Kirk: Dude, I just walked by Lindsay with a plate of donuts and she completely ignored me.

Riyanne: Doesn't surprise me. She is working on closing the accounts receivable for this quarter and has a bad case of the one-yard stare.

onion booty

Booty that looks so good it makes a grown man want to cry.

Damn, man, that girl's got onion booty.

or the terrorists have won

The best excuse to get what you want.

Continue buying SUVs, or the terrorists have won.

Repeal the Constitution, or the terrorists have won.

Dance naked in front of me, or the terrorists have won.

outside

An uncomfortable place where there's this big hot thing in the sky and there are other people you sometimes have to talk to.

I don't want to go outside.

Pac-Manning

To drive right on the dotted white lane divider, which gives the same effect as Pac-Man eating dots.

Dude, quit Pac-manning, you're gonna hit that car!

page clicker

An ebook that is exciting to read and hard to put down.

I found Neil deGrasse Tyson's autobiography with his personal account of the events of September 11, 2001, to be a real page clicker. I became absorbed with the story.

pants

1. Short for "underpants." British slang.

I've been wandering around my flat all day in only my pants.

2. To pull down someone's pants, trousers, or skirt. Short for "depants." Also "debag."

While I was talking to some girls, my so-called friend came up behind me and pantsed me.

3. To inflict a crushing defeat on someone.

Our team got pantsed again.

4. To crush someone with criticism.

Don't make silly comments in an Internet discussion group or you will be publicly pantsed.

5. Rubbish. Worthless. Nonsense. British slang.

Your opinion is pants. No one wants to hear it.

parade maker

A driver and/or car that goes consistently under the speed limit, causing a backup of many cars, a lot of frustration, and the inability to be where you want to be on time.

Gee, boss, I'm very sorry that I'm ten minutes late, but I was in a long line of cars stuck behind this parade maker.

parade wave

A slight hand gesture used to wave for prolonged periods of time (like during a parade), or as a casual nonverbal greeting to friends. With the arm bent at the elbow, the waver turns their wrist back and forth, exposing the front and then the back of the hand in a single motion.

I didn't feel like talking, so I gave her a quick parade wave as I walked by.

parking karma

The uncanny ability to find an open parking space in a desirable location of a busy parking lot.

I always have to park out in the boonies, but when I ride with Paul we're always in the front row. He's got some great parking karma.

passenger brake

The nonexistent brake pedal on the floor of the passenger (shotgun) side of the front seat of your car. It is used instinctively by the passenger when the driver is driving insanely too fast, and the car needs to come quickly to a stop, which may not seem very possible at that particular moment. It is sometimes used in conjunction with the "oh-shit handle" by the passenger door.

Doris was using her passenger brake all the freaking way here. She's the one who made us late by taking so long to get ready!

peasantvision

Television channels you get without a cable or satellite TV subscription.

I can't afford digital cable, but I still get some good shows with the rabbit ears on peasantvision.

pedexterity

The ability to pick up things with your feet.

Susie dropped her pencil on the floor during school and, thanking Sweet Jesus for her pedexterity, slipped her foot out of her flip-flop and picked it up with her toes.

peen

A derogatory term used to denote someone who is annoying. Short for "penis."

Joe always snores and keeps me up. He is a peen.

pen you in

A play on the phrase "pencil you in" but adds additional emphasis on the intention of the commitment.

Remley: Hey, wanna get some sushi tomorrow?

Erica: Most def. I will pen you in.

penny it forward

To leave your leftover penny or pennies from unwanted change at the counter of a convenience store.

Clerk: Mister, don't you want the rest of your change?

Me: Nah, just penny it forward.

perfectionist paralysis

The inability to start on a project, assignment, essay, or any creative task due to the fear of not getting it perfectly right.

Joe: You haven't started writing your paper yet?

Bob: Nope.

Joe: Isn't it due tomorrow?

Bob: Yep.

Joe: I thought you went to the library and did your research, made your notes, and wrote your outline.

Bob: Yep. I've got perfectionist paralysis.

phone grope

Grabbing at pockets, patting yourself down to make sure you have your cell phone and don't need to turn around and go back home for it. This behavior tends to be heightened in people who also have a habit of going back to check the locks on the doors several times before leaving home.

Magnus: Dude, stop that.

Derrick: What?

Magnus: Quit the phone grope. You're always grabbing at your pockets as soon as we're on the road. Didn't you remember your cell?

photobomb

To drop into someone else's photo, unexpectedly, right before it is taken.

Sarah: Hey, why is Jimmy in the background of our prom picture?

Ryan: idk, he must have photobombed it.

pi time

The time of the day when a digital clock reads 3:14.

Guy 1: Dude, what time is?

Guy 2: Dude, it's pi time.

pillow lust

That feeling that college students experience in which they feel so exhausted that the idea of their face hitting their pillow sounds so utterly fantastic, it's almost sexual.

Oh dude, it's been such a long week. I've got pillow lust, and I've got it bad.

pirate bath

Washing just the arm pit area and the private area with a wash cloth or handful of water. The easy definition is "pits and privates."

Kyle was in a helluva hurry and didn't have time to take a full shower. He instead took a pirate bath, and he was on his way.

pisshap

A mishap generally involving the mass consumption of alcohol and a misdirection of urine to an area other than the toilet. Can also apply to any other misadventure in some way linked to piss.

Man, Mark was so wasted at his birthday party last weekend that he woke up in the middle of the night and peed all over his computer. It was quite the pisshap.

pixel counting

Staring at one's screen to avoid bullshit at work.

Yeah, I missed the big catastrophe at work today as I was too busy pixel counting.

podestrian

A person who wears the iconic white standard iPod earbuds in their ears.

I saw three podestrians just waiting for a bus. They're everywhere!

polarpoint presentation

When the temperature in a conference or meeting room is turned way down to ensure that no one will be able to nod off during a meeting.

Harrison: Man, is the temperature in that room hosed again? My fingers were numb by the end of that staff meeting!

Noah: Nah, I saw them jack the temperature down about 20 degrees right before the meeting started. Bob will lull everyone to sleep unless they make it a polarpoint presentation.

police chase

When motorists are afraid to pass a police car while driving on a highway due to a fear of being caught for speeding. Similar to a parade maker. The result is a traffic jam.

Joe: Why is traffic moving soooo slowly?

Bob: Can't you see? We're in the middle of a police chase.

pooformance anxiety

Anxiety concerning the act of defecation, most often related to pooping in public restrooms.

I was at the game and I waited in line for a stall forever, but when I finally got in there I got pooformance anxiety and I couldn't go.

pop a squat

To sit down or to take a seat.

Yo, pop a squat over here.

porn moment

A move to initiate sexual or pseudo-sexual congress with someone that is so smooth it could only otherwise have happened in a heavily scripted porn film.

Dad: So I lean over to try and get her number and BAM, next thing I know we're doing it in the back of my van. It was such a porn moment.

Son: Uhh, thanks, Dad.

porn storm
Surfing for porn and getting bombarded with pop-up windows.

I tried to mouse off last night but I kept getting caught in a porn storm.

pornacopia
An overabundace of porn.

Jerry has a virtual pornacopia under his bed.

pornament
A pornographic Christmas ornament.

Somehow, Rodney's Christmas tree, decked out in garish purple lights and Mrs. Santa pornaments, failed to convey the solemnity and dignity of this holiest of days.

pornfolio
The mass of porn that one has stored on their computer, generally in a separate folder.

Damn, dude, I got 117 porn mpegs in my pornfolio.

post-acquaintance friend request
The friend request sent right after meeting someone for the first time.

After meeting Ryan at the party, Dave sent him a post-acquaintance friend request to secure their friendship.

postmodem depression

The feeling you get when you haven't had access to the Internet (i.e., Facebook and Twitter) for a long time, like several minutes.

(A family is on vacation)

Mom: Johnny, come to dinner!

Johnny: Fucking not hungry!

Mom (to Dad): What the hell is wrong with him?

Dad: He's got postmodem depression; he can't update his Facebook status.

Mom: But we have only been here for fifteen minutes.

powerdisking

Watching several episodes of a TV show in a row, usually from a DVD box set. This can be done over several evenings, or a marathon weekend.

I missed the first three seasons of Mad Men, *so I spent the past two weekends powerdisking all the episodes in order to be up to date for the premiere of the next season this month.*

powerpuff presentation

A PowerPoint presentation containing lots of flashy animations, cool pictures, and all sorts of other snazzy gimmicks, but almost entirely lacking in any real substance.

Tom: Didn't the VP's presentation just blow you away? I loved the falling apples turning into dollar bills.

Paul: But what was the point?

Tom: Dunno. It was definitely a powerpuff presentation, but those apples. . . .

precop

Short for pre-copulation. A mutually binding agreement (usually verbal) by and between consenting adults prior to engaging in casual sex. The agreement stipulates that all involved parties are exonerated from emotional attachment, postcoital contact, and any promise of future sex. Any and all disputes arising from said contract should be submitted and negotiated through binding arbitration. This agreement must involve a minimum of two individuals, with the maximum number to be determined in practical application.

Max: So, you stud, are you going to call Tina today?

Steve: No, I believe that would be a violation of our precop.

pregret

To regret something you're about to do anyway.

Every Friday night, I pregret that I will go to the club. I know I will stand there like an idiot and won't talk enough game to bring anyone home with me.

pre-hab

Where people go to avoid a future addiction.

Britney's kids are now in pre-hab.

premake

The original version of a song that another band has made a remake of, often used in a sarcastic manner.

My friend told me "Live and Let Die" was his favorite Guns N' Roses song, and he seemed surprised when I told him Paul McCartney had done a premake of that song.

premature evacuation

Getting caught while sneaking away after a one-night stand. Alternate: an early post-sex exit, i.e., before your partner is deep asleep.

He hooked up with some girl last night and got busted for a premature evacuation.

premature exasperation

Becoming upset about something before knowing all (or any) of the details.

When my parents found out I had been in an accident, my father's premature exasperation kicked in. He freaked out before hearing that some drunkard had rear-ended me at a red light.

premature joculation

Celebrating an event before it has been fully resolved. Sometimes quickly followed by an embarrassing retraction when things turn out differently.

The Pulp Fiction *quote (by the Winston Wolf character) "Well, let's not start sucking each other's dicks quite yet" is a great example of cautioning against premature joculation.*

P

pre-pull

Pulling the car door handle at the moment the driver unlocks the door, rendering the attempt fruitless, and resulting in minor frustration and/or embarrassment.

Could you unlock it again, dude? I pre-pulled.

presponse

To respond to a question before it is finished, often confusing the asker.

Wendy: So are you avail—

Jimmy: No.

Wendy: —able Monday?

(Silence)

Wendy: Are you?

pretext

To pretend to text someone in order to avoid awkward face-to-face situations. This happens most often when talking to someone you don't really know, or when you don't want to look weird while waiting for the bus.

My crush, Addie, and I have run out of things to talk about, so I will pretext to avoid any awkward silences.

prevert

A soft-core pervert. Someone who is in the early stages of perversion.

He was drawing naked women on his school homework, the little prevert.

procrasturbating

Using masturbation to otherwise occupy yourself while pressing matters await.

I had a paper due today, but I spent all night procrasturbating, so fuck that noise.

productive procrastination

Doing stuff to keep busy while avoiding what really needs doing. When all is said and done, your room is clean, your laundry is folded—but you haven't started your English paper.

I should really do my program. But instead, I think it's time for some productive procrastination. . . . Where's the mop?

professional celebrity

A famous person who has no discernable talent other than being famous.

Paris Hilton is a professional celebrity.

professional student

Person who receives multiple degrees and keeps taking courses instead of holding a profession related to the degrees earned. Can be a compliment or an insult depending on the speaker.

(As a compliment) Man, I think you're so cool for writing a dissertation on Mesoamerican maize fertilization. You're a real professional student!

(As an insult) Hey Jack, won't you get a real job and quit being a professional student?

props

Short for "proper recognition."

I had to give him props for sleeping with that smokin' hot girl, Vanessa, even though she's my girlfriend.

proximity infatuation

An infatuation that develops out of close-quarters operation with another person.

Randall: I swear I'm in love with this girl from philosophy class. I've been sitting next to her for like three weeks, and it's obvious we're meant for each other.

Sweeney: Well, do you know anything else about her? I bet you've just made up a life outside of class for her in your head. You're getting caught up in a shortsighted proximity infatuation, man; just wait a couple weeks after class is over and you won't even remember her.

puma

An attractive woman in her late twenties or early thirties. She is a precougar/urban cougar.

I think that puma just grabbed my ass.

purchase pleasure

The unexplained feeling of bliss, joy, and satisfaction one gets following a purchase. It can last from a few hours to a few weeks depending on the size, worth, or usefulness of the item acquired. Buyer's remorse can sometimes follow or replace purchase pleasure. It is often a reason for shopping addiction.

Laura: Hanging out and shopping with you yesterday made me really happy.

Grant: Me too, but then I'm always happy when I buy things. I'm still getting purchase pleasure today.

purge the cabin
To roll the windows down on a vehicle for some fresh air, usually after one of the passengers has passed gas.

Gawd damn was that foul! Purge the cabin before we suffocate back here!

puzzle butt
The crack in a monopoly board.

The dice landed right on the puzzle butt.

P

quarter-life crisis

Refers to the numerous personal crises brought on by entering adulthood and being expected to become a responsible, productive member of society. Characterized by first gray hairs/wrinkles, excessive drinking, hanging out with people who are younger in order to feel younger again only to end up looking creepy, extreme fear of all of these things. Also a "midyouth crisis."

Wow, paying back these student loans is really a bitch. They are not helping my quarter-life crisis one bit. . . . Time to put on my tie and go sit in my cube and play solitaire—I mean, work.

question fart

A fart that sounds as if the inflection raises toward its end, exactly as you would do with your voice when asking a question.

Barry punctuated his statement with a tiny question fart.

quick question

A question that usually requires a long answer. A close relative of the stupid question and the rhetorical question.

Joan: I have a quick question for you. How do you solve for "x" in this complex differential equation?

Bob: Uhhhhhh. . . .

reader's block

Related to writer's block, this is when you cannot, for the life of you, pick up a book and read it. Sure, you may be able to read a paragraph or two, or maybe even a page, but you don't retain anything of what you just read or have the attention span and/or will to go on.

This is common for those who have ADD, are in possession of garbage literature, or are just so exhausted from having to read so many books during school/college that reading anything else, even for pleasure, has become impossible. To those who love to read, this is worse than heart disease and cancer combined.

Eddie: Hey, man, I see you're reading McCarthy's The Road. *Nice.*

Nerdlinger: I'm trying to read it, but I got this damn reader's block! I'm twenty pages in, but I don't remember anything. Fuck!

Eddie: Poor bastard.

reality challenged

A state in which one is utterly and completely unable to distinguish fact from fiction, and is thus obviously and undeniably full of shit.

That politician is SO reality challenged that he can't even tell shit from Shinola!

rebooty

A booty call made with an ex, or a renewed relationship with an ex.

After they broke up, Joe still called Kate for some rebooty on weekends.

rebound job

A job you take knowing that it isn't long term, often due to an emergency situation in which you know you're going to lose your current job. It provides a paycheck while you take your time looking for a better job.

Starbucks was totally a rebound job—I was minutes from getting fired and needed something fast!

recessionitis

An excuse for not doing anything because you simply can't afford it. Much like other itises, it can take months or even years to go away.

Amber: Hey, are you coming out to the bar tonight?

Amy: Ahh, man, I wish I could . . . but I have a really bad case of recessionitis.

recrap

To sum up a discussion composed largely of useless bullshit.

Trish: Tell me how the staff meeting went.

Allie: Allow me to recrap. . . .

recyclopath

A person who militantly engages in recycling and is so hostile to simply throwing away garbage that it borders on mental illness. Also a pejorative for an extreme environmentalist.

Leigh pees in a bucket and uses it to water and fertilize her garden— what a recyclopath!

refrigerator blindness

Selective loss of visual acuity in association with common foraging of the refrigerator. Predominantly seen in children and males.

Matt: Honey, where's the orange juice?

Christina: Are you blind? Second shelf on the right!

Matt: Sorry, must be that pesky refrigerator blindness again. . . .

R

regret ceiling

The point at which one stops feeling remorseful regarding a thought, comment, or action.

I hit the regret ceiling last night regarding comments I made about Jody's weight several weeks ago. Her fat ass just needs to get over it.

remasculate

The opposite of emasculate. To grow one's balls back after they have been shrunken by an especially effeminate activity.

God, the girlfriend dragged me to go see License to Wed. *It was terrible. I had to remasculate afterwards by watching* Die Hard: The Bloody Retribution.

remote dance

The movements you make with your hand when trying to get your TV to recognize your remote control. All remote dances are different, but most involve twisting your hand around until the remote is almost upside down, thinking that for some reason that will help.

Last night, I remote danced for about five minutes just trying to turn the volume up.

renob

"Boner" spelled backward. A less derogatory way to call someone a boner.

Justin is a total renob today.

rent-a-cop

Security guards, usually unarmed, who are hired by companies and rented out to agencies for things such as concerts or school security.

My school is full of rent-a-cops, armed with nothing tougher than their cell phones. Safe, it ain't!

rescue chip

The chip you use to fish the bits of the first one that broke apart in the dip.

My tortilla chip busted when I tried to load it with extra salsa, so I gotta get a rescue chip.

reserection

A morning wood of biblical proportions.

On the third day, Jesus awoke from the tomb with a raging reserection.

resolution rush

The rush of people who swarm the gym and other exercise places in the first weeks of the year. Usually subsides quickly.

The gym's got the resolution rush, but will be clear by Valentine's Day.

restless-lip syndrome

When a person keeps interrupting a conversation and can't keep their mouth shut.

Chris has to come to my house to drink because when we're at his house Linda's restless-lip syndrome prevents us from carrying on a conversation.

retard in aluminum foil

What a lady's knight in shining armor becomes when she really gets to know him.

R

I thought he was my knight in shining armor. Turns out, he was just a retard in aluminum foil!

retox

To start consuming drugs and alcohol again after a hiatus in an effort to avoid the effects of withdrawal.

Man, I haven't had a drink since Monday, and I'm getting the shakes. I'd better retox.

ride VIP

To ride in the backseat of a car even when the front passenger seat is available.

Tommy: Do you want to sit up front?

Tony: No, it's cool. I'm gonna ride VIP.

ridin' qwerty

Texting while driving where it's illegal.

Hey, sorry I couldn't reply to your SMS. I was ridin' qwerty.

ridonkulous

Completely absurd and laughable. Term popularized by the fictional character Seth Cohen on the TV show *The O.C.*

Deserving or inspiring ridicule to the highest degree.

The number of dead hookers in the apartment was redonkulous.

rigor mortgage

The feeling that sets in when you realize the value of your house is approaching zero.

Ron: How do you feel about the halted construction in your neighborhood?

Dave: I'm stiff with rigor mortgage.

ringtone DJ

A person who shuffles through all their ringtones, one after another, annoying the people around them. You could yell at them, but they wouldn't stop.

Jordan: Hey, Ringtone DJ, I don't wanna hear your tones. Stop showing off, jackass.

Ringtone DJ: Hey, do you like this one? It's "I Wanna 1-2-1 with You."

robocracy

A government run by robots. They will be able to lie and have scandals more efficiently than humans.

Vote Candidatebot 4000 in 2012 or be processed for organs.

rock out with my Spock out

To openly be a fan of any of the *Star Trek* TV series and/ or films.

Nerd 1: Did you hear about the Star Trek *marathon tonight?*

Nerd 2: Affirmative, Captain. I'm gonna rock out with my Spock out.

rockstar parking

Parking in the closest spot available to your destination (not including handicapped designated areas), or parking right next to the door or the building.

Check out my rockstar parking!

roommate chicken

Game played by a group of people sharing a living space in which each tries to avoid doing a household chore for an extended period because each believes it's someone else's responsibility. The idea is that eventually the situation will reach a critical mass, causing the guilty party to cave in and do the chore. In practice, the situation can escalate to extreme levels.

Bobby: I'm not going to do the dishes. It's your turn.

Nick: Yeah, but 90 percent of them are from the dinner you made for your girlfriend. I'm not cleaning up your mess.

Bobby: I'm not playing roommate chicken with you on this. Clean it up!

Nick: I'll die before I clean your mess.

Bobby: Fuck you!

Nick: Fuck you!

run and tell that

To go spread the word. To let it be known. After Antoine Dodson, a young hero from Huntsville, Alabama, who saved his sister from an attack and gave a public message to the media for the perp, letting him know that this wasn't the end of the story, and that he would be caught.

Antoine: You don't have to confess. . . . We looking for you. We gon' find you. . . . So you can run and tell that, homeboy!

running latte

Showing up late to work because you stopped for coffee along the way.

I told them I got stuck in traffic, but really I was running latte.

Russian toilette

After sitting on the toilet, you notice that there is less than one quarter of a roll of toilet paper, and no spare in the bathroom. You decide to go anyway, gambling on the fact you will have enough toilet paper to have a satisfying wipe.

Husband: Honey, I just played Russian toilette and lost.

Wife: Sucks to be you. Try not to bite your fingernails.

R

sacrelicious

A description of a recipe that should not exist for religious reasons, but tastes good anyway. Or, any cooking done with communion wafers.

Try some Matzo crackers and bacon dip—it's sacrelicious.

safe sexting

Using a password or other safety feature to prevent your friends, parents, girlfriends, etc., from discovering the assortment of hot or racy pictures on your cell, computer, email, or other encryptable devices.

Girl 1: I dunno, should I send John this pic?

Girl 2: It's fine—John practices safe sexting!

Girl 1: That's good. No way that this pic will get into the wrong hands if he is safe sexting.

salsa fucked

Phenomenon that occurs when dining at a Mexican restaurant with a large group and the salsa is not distributed evenly throughout the table. The areas of the table that do not have ample amounts of salsa are "salsa fucked."

Trace: Jeff, all of the salsa is at the other end of the table, yo.

Jeff: I know, we got salsa fucked.

salty

Unusually grumpy or cross. In a bad mood. Unfriendly or hostile.

Aaron is salty tonight; he isn't getting along with anyone.

sammich

A sandwich, with connotations of extra goodness. For example, if you pour gravy on a roast beef sandwich, you then have a roast beef sammich.

Subway sells sandwiches, but I'd rather go home and make a sammich.

sapiosexual

One who finds intelligence the most sexually attractive feature.

I want an incisive, inquisitive, insightful, irreverent mind. I want someone for whom philosophical discussion is foreplay. I want someone who sometimes makes me go "ouch!" due to their wit and evil sense of humor. I want someone whom I can reach out and touch randomly. I want someone I can cuddle with. I guess I'm just a sapiosexual.

Sarah Palin effect

The idea that expertise on a certain subject can be gained through geographical proximity to it.

Sarah Palin proclaimed herself an expert on foreign affairs with Russia due to Alaska's proximity to Russia, and the Sarah Palin effect was born.

screen saver

The blank expression that comes across a person's face when they are daydreaming.

Bradley: Dude, check out Dave daydreaming; he looks miles away.

Tabitha: Yeah mate, I know, he has his screen saver on.

screwvenir

Anything you keep (whether stolen or given to you) from someone's house after you've slept with them.

Laura didn't really like doing it with Chip so much, but she did nab a copy of Time *magazine with Mick Jagger on it from his house as a screwvenir.*

selective fatigue syndrome

What you really have when you use fatigue as an excuse because you don't want to perform undesirable tasks, such as work.

My coworker claimed her chronic fatigue syndrome kept her from coming to work, but she had no problems making it to the nightclubs. What she really has is selective fatigue syndrome.

self-first

The rule you use to get out of the "bros before hoes" rule. Only to be used when there is more than an 80 percent chance of you getting laid.

I know our rule is bros befo' hoes, but you see that girl all up on me? It's self-first tonight. Sorry, playa.

self-helpless

Unable to deal with life. People with this condition are usually found sitting around a neglected apartment with bad hair and a bad outfit.

I saw Kenny at our high school reunion. He's still living with his parents and saving up for a Camaro . . . totally self-helpless.

senioritis

A crippling disease that strikes high school seniors. Symptoms include laziness and an excessive wearing of track pants, old athletic shirts, sweatpants, athletic shorts, and sweatshirts. Also features a lack of studying, repeated absences, and a generally dismissive attitude. The only known cure is a phenomenon known as graduation.

Andy: Why didn't you study for your math test, Kuhns?

Kuhns: Oh, who studies for a math test, anyways? I got senioritis.

serial chiller

A person who always kicks back and relaxes. One who rarely shoulders responsibility and avoids stress and anxiety.

Jake is either grafted to the couch, the backyard hammock, the lounge chair, or the La-Z-Boy . . . or he's still in bed. I envy that serial chiller.

severance lay

When, after ending a relationship, you have sex for the last time.

My girlfriend is moving out of town, so we're splitting up. I'm swinging by her apartment tonight to get my stuff and my severance lay.

sex without the X

Dull, lifeless, boring, unexciting lovemaking, as in non-X-rated sex.

A day without sunshine is like sex without the X.

sexercism

Having sex with someone new to get over someone old. A way to cut any last emotional ties to a person you used to have sex with. A nonreligious, therapeutic exercise.

Person 1: She needs to get over her ex already!

Person 2: Yeah, she needs a sexercism real fast.

sexile

To banish a roommate from the room/dorm/apartment so that one can engage in intimate relations with one's significant other/sex partner.

My roommate is gonna sexile me on Valentine's Day so that he and Yolanda can have their hot monkey sex in our room.

sexting

Text messaging someone in the hopes of having a sexual encounter with them later. Initially casual, it transitions into highly suggestive and even sexually explicit messages.

(Sexting in action)

Nancy: Wut do u want?

Bob: Cum over to my place now.

Nancy: Is NE1 else there?

Bob: No. I need to c u.

Nancy: K. Will b there soon.

shart

Blend of "shit" and "fart." A small, unintended defecation that occurs when one relaxes to fart.

I sharted at the party last night and went home pronto to change my clothes.

Shatner commas

Oddly placed commas that don't seem to serve any actual purpose in punctuation but make it look like you should take odd pauses, as William Shatner does when delivering lines.

When, we get to, the restaurant, we should, order some, tasty, beverages.

sheeple

People who are unable to think for themselves. Followers. Lemmings.

All the teens were wearing bell-bottoms because they were sheeple.

shelf esteem

When someone builds their self-esteem from self-help books.

My coworker just added Dr. Phil to her shelf-esteem library. Now every day at lunch it's Dr. P said this, Dr. P said that.

shirt mask

The part of the shirt located just below the chin and used to filter foul odors, such as in unclean bathrooms, or after a destructive passing of gas (fart, chemical attack).

Duuude . . . that truck stop restroom was so narsty I had to use my shirt mask just to take a piss.

shit just got real

An expression used when a joking or friendly conversation suddenly takes a turn for the worse and escalates toward a hostile situation and/or a physical scuffle.

Tommy: I have never been so tired in my life.

George: That's what your mom said last night.

Random yell from someone not actually involved: SHIT JUST GOT REAL!

S

shitload

More than an assload, but less than a fuckton.

I have a shitload of beer, but down at my friend's place, they have a whole fuckton.

shiznit

The greatest, in a certain category or universally.
Phenomenal, biotch! Also "shiznat."

*Damn, Tony! Your new ride is the shiznit! Lemme borrow it to drive
by Mya's.*

shopping window

The time period during which a guy is actually engaged
in the shopping experience. This period can last from
almost no time at all to literally hours for a metrosexual,
and includes all forms of shopping, from the grocery store
to designer boutiques. It should also be noted that this
period can be increased through witty girl techniques such
as handing a guy a BlackBerry loaded with BrickBreaker to
play, or sitting him in front of a couch with SportsCenter.

*I am totally down to go try on a few pairs of jeans right now, but I
am letting you know that my shopping window is only about forty-five
minutes today.*

short story long

Phrase used when a story could have been told in a more
concise way but is dragged out because the teller doesn't
know how to tell a story. It's a play on the annoying clarifier
"Long story short," which really never seems to be that
short, anyway.

*So I was walking into the store the other day—I wanted to get some
aspirin because I had this massive headache—and I walked down
aisle four, but they only had Tylenol, but that doesn't work, and I
went to the counter and, short story long, this guy was holding up the
store!*

shower tissue

When you're in a shower and have to blow your nose. You use your index and thumb and replicate the actions of blowing your nose, then let the shower wash the boogers away.

Man, the other day I shower tissued and it flew onto my face!

shuffle shame

When your MP3 music player is playing on speakers in shuffle mode and somebody enters the room at the exact moment the worst song of your collection is being played.

I felt shuffle shame when Tony came to the office today and Paris Hilton's single came on.

shut up and keep talking

An expression that's used when you want information from someone but that someone keeps telling boring details you don't need to know. Can be emphasized by using "Shut the fuck up and keep talking," instead.

Riley: So we went to her bedroom, and there were a lot of dolls there. She also had a poster of—

Emmet: Dude, shut up and keep talking. Did anything happen?

shyPod

Hesitant to share the contents of one's iPod.

Because Doug downloaded Britney Spears's "Toxic" he was totally shyPod when Dru wanted to take a peek at his library.

sideboob

A view of the female breast seen from a side, generally under loosely fitting clothes. Very titillating and sexual without showing any overt nudity.

My brother's g/f's sideboob totally distracted me from my own g/f.

silent rave

"Rave" or form of wild dancing party where all of the members listen to music through headphones on separate portable music players. The players are all synchronized so everyone is hearing the same thing, but no outsiders hear anything.

The police didn't bust the silent rave down the street because nobody complained about the noise.

singletasker

The opposite of multitasker, a singletasker is one who only takes upon one task at a time and follows it through to completion. Often used sarcastically when someone is bragging about their supreme multitasking skills.

Bobby: Today I'm only going to focus on finishing my TPS reports and not answer the phone, email, text, IM, staple, and make breakfast simultaneously.

Jeffy: You are such the singletasker!

Bobby: I can't even respond to you at this time, because then I'd be multitasking.

sinlaws

The parents of your live-in boyfriend/girlfriend.

I am having my sinlaws over for dinner. . . . I hope I make a good impression, since I have been shacking up with their son for a few weeks now, and they are not down with the fact we are living in sin.

sketch

Uncertain or potentially bad, like a party that is to happen in the future but there are rumors of the cops already knowing about it.

I don't wanna go if it's gonna be sketch.

slacktivism

Participating in obviously pointless activities as an expedient alternative to actually expending effort to fix a problem.

Signing an email petition to stop rampant crime is slacktivism. Want to really make your community safer? Get off your ass and start a neighborhood watch!

sleep drunk

When you're woken up from a nap and your mental state of confusion resembles that of a drunken person.

When that crazy bitch tried to crawl into bed with me, I was too sleep drunk to say no.

sleep slut

One who sleeps frequently and can accumulate excess hours of sleep above and beyond the mean. Sleep sluts are able to fall asleep indiscriminately and value sleep above all else.

Within minutes of boarding the commuter train, Mark was fast asleep. Mark's sleep-slut powers were legendary, and he was always able to wake before his stop.

slide

A person you mess around with outside of a relationship but are not serious about.

Nah, son, she ain't my girl—she's just a slide.

slip of the thumbs

Error in sending a text message when the actual recipient of the message is not the intended recipient. Can happen when you try to reply to one person, and another message comes in just as you're about to reply, and you end up replying to the wrong person. Can have detrimental effects.

Girlfriend to married guy: Hey, what are you up to?

(Guy is getting ready to reply, when he's distracted for two seconds, during which time the following message hits his phone:)

Wife to husband: I made it to Dallas.

Husband to his wife (in a slip of the thumbs): Nothing, my wife is out of town if you want to sleep over tonight.

Wife to husband: WTF!?!?!

slore

Cross between "slut" and "whore." A woman who indiscriminately shares a bed with anyone who shows interest, often without protection and/or discretion.

Person 1: They're saying that chick who sued him was also with other guys that night.

Person 2: What a slore.

sloth cloth

An old T-shirt you wear while hanging around the house.

The great man came to the door wearing baggy boxer shorts and a food-stained sloth cloth.

slow burn

An insult that doesn't sink in for a while.

He's an idiot; you can say any sort of shit to his face and it'll be a slow burn. He won't figure it out for days.

slow your roll

1. Slow down. Be calm.

Slow your roll, homey! I'm tryin' to relax up in this mutha.

2. Slow down your game. Stop coming on so strong to a female.

You'd better slow your roll, junior player. You'll just get shut down going like that.

slurring your text

When you're so drunk that your texts are unreadable.

(310): heryls so imsd gaonna bea tah the apartty tognlaoit!!!!

(510): chris, u gotta stop slurring your texts.

smartphone shuffle

The act of walking slowly or shuffling because you're too preoccupied with tasks being done on your smartphone such as browsing the Internet, texting, etc. The smartphone shuffle can sometimes be a danger to oneself, such as when crossing a road. It can also be a nuisance for other people, as distracted smartphone shufflers block hallways, stairs, or sidewalks, and impede the flow of pedestrian traffic.

Stop doing the smartphone shuffle! You're blocking the sidewalk.

smell check

Double-checking the clothes you put on for any funky odors before getting dressed and leaving the house.

Damn, homeboy should have run a smell check on his pants before he came to work today. Dude smells like funky taint.

snap

Interjection used to express a feeling of excitement, surprise, disappointment, or extreme satisfaction, depending on the context. Alternative to "aw, damn," "aw, shit."

Oh, snap, the engine's on fire!

Check out the jelly shakin' on her as she drops it to the floor. Snap!

I was like "snap" when I saw them rolling this way.

snarf

When one is eating or drinking and is provoked by something funny that causes them to laugh and expel food or drink out of the nasal passages or mouth.

Dude, I was eating my lunch at school and this chick said something hilarious and I totally snarfed sandwich all over the place.

snark

Combination of "snide" and "remark." Sarcastic comment(s).

His commentary was rife with snark.

Her snarky remarks had half the room on the floor laughing, and the other half ready to walk out.

"Your boundless ineptitude is astounding," she snarkily declared.

sniff test

To smell an item of already-worn clothing to see whether it is suitable to wear out. Common among students who can't be bothered to do their washing.

Friend 1: Hey, man, can't you just wear those boxers?

Friend 2: (sniff test) Yeah, I can get a couple more uses out of these.

snot rocket

When you plug one nostril with your finger and blow out of the other nostril with everything you have, sending a snot projectile out of the nose.

Without tissue, all I could do to clear my nose was to blow a snot rocket.

snow hysteria

When the populace's fear of a snowstorm creates traffic jams and general panic way before any flakes even fall. Usually turns out to be a totally disproportionate response to a minor snowstorm.

Everyone is fleeing the office thanks to snow hysteria . . . but it isn't supposed to start snowing until 9 p.m.

soap grafting

Attaching an almost completely used piece of soap to a new, unused piece because it is now too small to be conveniently used but you also don't want to waste it.

My mom always soap grafts because she doesn't want to waste anything. Soap grafting is good.

social chameleon

Someone who changes the way they interact with people depending on whom they're with.

Chris is such a social chameleon. He's a nice guy at chess club, but such a dick on the football team.

social fruitfly

Like a social butterfly, but without any charm or beauty. An unwanted pest.

My manager is a social fruitfly. All he does is talk and never does any work.

social notworking

The practice of spending time unproductively on social-networking websites, especially when one should be working.

Joe: Hey, Mark is constantly updating his Facebook status; does he not have any work to do?

John: His company obviously doesn't realize how much social notworking he is doing!

social terrorism

When someone you know comes to visit unexpectedly and inconveniently, often staying for a long time, and you can't tell them to leave without being rude.

Yesterday, I was just about to go out, and then the doorbell rang. It was Sally, and she invited herself in and stayed for an hour! It was social terrorism!

Solitaire denial

Flipping through the deck over and over while playing the card game Solitaire even though there are no more moves available, denying that you have lost even though you already know it.

Denny: Dude, you've gone through the deck three times already. Give it up; you've lost.

Colin: . . . So I have. I'm in solitaire denial again.

some-sex marriage

A marriage in which a couple participates in minimal sexual activity.

Bill and Wanda have a some-sex marriage. They're pretty much down to just birthdays and Valentine's Day.

song bingeing

To binge on a song or artist, obsessively listening over a relatively short period of time. Periods of song bingeing are followed by extended periods of skipping the same track or artist.

Tiffany: OMG, I'm so bloody obsessed with Fall Out Boy's new song!! I've played it eighty-four times in the last twenty-four hours!!

Brent: Stop song bingeing and go listen to other shit for once.

sore winner

Someone who wins and spends far too much time gloating over it, to the point that the rest of the people feel poorly about even participating.

Ali was a sore winner when he sang "We Are the Champions" after winning the NCAA bracket.

soundbitten

When a sound bite of a statement is used to make someone look like an idiot, a racist, a fool, etc.

Man, did you hear that Romney quote on The Daily Show *last night? He should know better than to let himself get soundbitten like that.*

sounds like my first time

Phrase used in the same way as "That's what he said." By definition, this refers to the first time one engaged in sexual intercourse.

Luana (referring to something non sexual): I don't understand why the packaging is so tight.

Tara: Sounds like my first time.

spank bank

A memorable collection of mental images that one wishes to retain for master debational purposes.

Reggie: Yo, 2 o'clock, see that thong?

Tony: Yeah, that's going in the spank bank.

spending amnesia

Trying to recall where and when you spent all your money. Normally when said money is needed. A product of bad spending habits and fucking awesome party nights.

Jesse: Dude, I'm so bad with money! It just disappears.

Nico: You might have spending amnesia. I remember you lost at beer pong, then hit the pubs with those trannies.

spicy edit

When telling a story to friends, you realize it isn't as cool as you thought it was when you started, and decide to edit it with exaggerations or lies to make it sound more interesting.

So I heard Lexi told Cassandra that she didn't like her anymore, and that's why they aren't talking . . . (spicy edit) . . . and also because she slept with her boyfriend.

spit take

A visual gimmick used in film and onstage in which a person is surprised or taken aback by another's actions or words while drinking, and spits or sputters that liquid.

He did a spit take when she told him she was pregnant.

sporking

Spooning, with the addition of an erection.

We fell asleep . . . then when I woke up in the morning, he was totally sporking me!

sporn

Combination of "spam" and "porn." What fills most email inboxes.

Matt anxiously checked his Hotmail inbox for relevant email from his honey, but alas, it was filled to the brim with unncessary sporn.

sport snob

Someone who believes that their vast and ultimately unnecessary knowledge of sports makes them a better sports watcher. They will often ridicule or speak condescendingly toward someone of lesser sports knowledge.

Louis: Wow! That was a great touchdown pass. . . .

Leo: That's what quarterbacks do . . . idiot. . . .

Louis: Don't be such a fucking sport snob.

spot tease

A parking spot that appears to be open, but is actually taken by a small car or motorcycle. Also can refer to a car that takes up 90 percent of its own spot and 10 percent of the one next to it, leaving no room for another car to park.

All right! Parking spot just two away from the mall! Wait . . . damn Smart Car's parked there! Stupid spot tease!

spring broke

When you're broke because you spent all your money on spring break.

Guy 1: Hey man, wanna go to a movie or somethin'?

Guy 2: Nah, I'm spring broke. The cash I took to Vegas, stayed in Vegas.

stall waiting

When you realize that you and your neighbor have finished using the bathroom at the same time so you delay exiting the stall a few seconds to avoid any uncomfortable eye contact or "excuse me"s while leaving the stall. Wait period is usually until the person reaches the buffer zone of the sink, where all normal social etiquettes are reactivated.

Hmm . . . Bob and I just flushed at the same time. I better do a little stall waiting.

status texting

When someone texts you completely random and/or insignificant information only pertaining to themselves, as if they were updating their Facebook status.

Lauren (via text): I'm taking pictures at my sister's wedding!!!
Grace (via text): Please, no status texting. Save that shit for Facebook.

staycation

A vacation spent at one's home enjoying all that one's home environs have to offer.

Even though I live and work in New York, I don't always get to enjoy all it has to offer, what with my work commitments; but I sure did have an awesome time here during my spring staycation.

stealth abs

When your ripped six-pack is covered by a thick layer of fat.

This isn't a beer belly; it's my stealth abs. I just needed to avoid attracting too many ladies with my well-defined stomach.

stealth bomber

Someone who breaks wind silently, then moves out of the room before anyone notices.

What the . . . ? Oh my God, do you smell that? Who's the stealth bomber?!

stealth-call

To call someone back, but you don't want to talk to them, so you wait until you know they can't talk and leave a voice mail.

I don't want to tell Karen I can't make it tonight, so I'll stealth-call her when she's on her flight and has her phone shut off.

steez

Style with ease. A person's unique style. How an individual carries himself.

You know I don't get down like that. You know my steez.

sticker paralysis

What happens when you have a really awesome sticker and no appropriate place to use it. General symptoms include keeping the sticker in a drawer and never using it. Sometimes when you do use it you have affixation remorse afterward.

I have contracted a case of sticker paralysis from this vintage Apple sticker. I can't decide if I should put it on my fake plastic guitar or my rear window or my skateboard. It is too precious to use on just anything.

sticker shock

A condition resulting from seeing the total price of a bunch of items and realizing the damage is much greater than you originally expected. May cause a person to have second thoughts about the purchase.

I wanted to book your mom for 7 days of her "services," but when I realized the total came to $21, I got major sticker shock and decided to bail out.

stoptional

When the braking of a car is left to one's choice due to an unnecessary stop sign.

Norah: Did you just blow through that stop sign?

Justin: Oh, no worries. It was stoptional.

store d'oeuvres

Snacks and food samples that a grocery store will serve at various locations in order to tempt the patrons into buying something they weren't planning to buy (pizza, chips and dip, sausage, etc.). Usually happens on the weekend.

I went to Costco the other day and filled up on store d'oeuvres.

strategic-dipping

When a chip (or other dippable food) is dipped, bitten, and then turned over so that the tainted, bitten, and saliva-covered part isn't able to corrupt the dip.

Don: Hey man, no double-dipping!

Mac: I'm not double-dipping! I'm strategic-dipping!

stress eater

Someone who, in reaction to high levels of stress, eats excessive amounts of food.

Denny: Damn, John just ate four hamburgers and downed a chocolate shake!

Leah: Yeah, he has been studying for finals all week.

Denny: Wow, that guy is a wicked stress eater.

suck

To be really, really crappy. "Sucks" is sometimes written as "sux."

That team last night really sucked. They just plain sucked. I've seen teams suck before, but they were the suckiest buncha sucks that ever sucked.

sugar honey iced tea

Stand-in for "SHIT" when you can't openly swear.

Oh, sugar honey iced tea, I didn't mean to do that!!

suicide doors

Suicide doors refer to car doors that open in the opposite of the regular direction—hinges are at the back, and the front of the door opens. Many cars before WWII had those, and now it is a popular conversion on tuned trucks. Suicide doors are considered far more dangerous than normal doors because of the possiblity of opening during movement.

I am thinking of converting my truck to suicide doors so I can take stuff in and out easier.

swole

Extremely muscular or buff.

Craig: Yo, Ray-Ray, have you seen Trey lately? He's been hittin' the weights, hasn't he? He's swole, dawg.

sympathy seeker

A person whose status updates on Facebook are solely for the purpose of gaining sympathy.

Johnny is such a sympathy seeker, he would go on Facebook to say that his pet rock died if it would get him some pity comments.

tab o' war

The fight over who will pay the check at the dinner table.

Sabine: You're being ridiculous, Debbie. I want to pay tonight.

Julie: Just give her the damn check, Sabine. You're having a tab o' war in the middle of the restaurant!

tag hag

A person who is obsessed with name-brand clothing. Also, label whore.

Nicole always flaunts the latest clothing. She is such a tag hag.

tanorexia

A disease in which no matter how tan a person is, they never think they are tan enough.

That girl needs to stay away from the tanning booth for a while; she looks positively tanorexic!

tattoo remorse

What you feel when you look at a tattoo you got when you were younger, or thought would be cool at the time, and you realize the tattoo is stupid and wish you had never gotten it.

Joe: My tattoo remorse is catching up on me after realizing getting my ex-wife's name, "Jessica," tattooed on my arm was just dumb.

John: Yeah, that looks just plain stupid now.

technolust

The constant desire to have the newest, flashiest, fastest, shiniest gadget available, even if the one you just bought is only two months old and still works great.

Your new iPhone makes me horny with uncontrollable technolust.

technosexual

A dandyish narcissist in love with not only himself but also his urban lifestyle and gadgets. A straight man who is in touch with his feminine side and has an extreme fondness for electronics such as cell phones, PDAs, computers, software, and the web.

You'd never believe it to look at him, but he's a technosexual!

testicular fortitude

Balls, guts, intestinal fortitude.

He lacked the testicular fortitude to stand up to his boss.

text purgatory

The time period one waits for a response to a flirtatious text.

Dave was in text purgatory after texting Kiri, "Drinks later?"

text support

Advice or encouragement delivered via text. Frequently related to dating and boss hating. Pronounced like tech support.

Hey, thanks for all the text support last night! I have a coffee date with him today.

text-hole

Someone who texts on their cell phone in really inappropriate places or at really inappropriate times, such as in movie theaters, at concerts or plays, or during sex.

The movie was great, except right during the best scene, this text-hole in front of me lit up his phone and started texting away.

text-killer

Phrases and words such as "lol yeah" and "haha ok" that are guaranteed to kill any text conversation.

Wren: r u coming 2 the prty 2nite?

Alex: no i cant cuz i hav 2 go 2 a family reunion

Wren: haha ok

Alex: way to use a text-killer . . . now wat do i say?

textlemming

People who walk while constantly texting—head down, can't see where they're going, at a greater risk of walking into things, such as moving cars and closed doors.

Hey, did you just see that textlemming walk right into that streetlamp?

textpectation

The anticipation one feels when waiting for a response to a text message.

I just texted her for a date, and now the textpectation is killing me.

textrovert

One who feels an increased sense of bravery when texting, as opposed to in person. One who will often only say what they really feel over text messages.

Kelly: So how'd the conversation go with Bill last night?

Wendy: Ah, he's such a textrovert. We didn't make any progress until I went home and he spilled his guts over texts.

textual intercourse

The consummation of a relationship via SMS messages.

Matt and Heather have been having textual intercourse for over a month.

textual satisfaction

The feeling you get when your phone has a new message/ missed call.

Dude, I've been getting textual satisfaction all day. I already have five new messages.

textually frustrated
When texting with someone over IM or SMS who takes too long to reply, leaving you waiting and frustrated.

Sara always leaves me textually frustrated. She takes forever!

Thanksgiving
Another excuse for Americans to spend an entire day eating.

William: Damn, it's not a weekend, and I want to eat all day.

Eliza: Why don't we invent a holiday, and give it a stupid name—like Thanksgiving?

William: Fo' shizzle, my pilgrizzle!

that's a good question
A phrase that indicates the speaker has absolutely no idea how to answer said question. Often used to stall for time.

Photography teacher walking in on students who should be at pep rally: What are you doing here?

Sally: That's a good question!

that's crazy
The perfect response when you haven't been listening at all. It works whether the other person has been saying something funny, or sad, or infuriating, or boring.

Todd: My girlfriend dumped me last night.

Ash (thirsty, not paying attention): Oh man, that's crazy.

Hunter: I won 500 bucks at craps last weekend.

Ash (hungry, daydreaming about a tasty sandwich, not listening): Wow, that's crazy.

that's how I roll

What someone would say to insinuate that something is their style, or the way they usually do things.

Remy: Yo man, so did you already hit it or what?

Taylor: Yeah, you know that's how I roll.

that's what BP said

A variant of "that's what she said." Instead of referring to sexual connotations, it is used to refer to spending a lot of money, making a mess, or fucking up very badly. Arose after the 2010 British Petroleum oil leak in the Gulf of Mexico.

Blake: Oh man, I really screwed the pooch on that one.

Yanic: That's what BP said!

Carla: It's going to take me all day to clean this mess up.

Marie: That's what BP said!

Cliff: I'm paying tonight. The sky is the limit.

José: That's what BP said!

the "fuck" word

Parody of the use of the phrase "the 'f' word" in place of "fuck." Typically used to express disdain or disregard for censorship.

leikomg canu believe I said the "fuck" word. lollers!

the book-off

When you get out a book on the train, tube, bus, or plane in order to avoid talking to the person next to you. Like a brush-off with a book.

Passenger 1: Blablabla, isn't the weather terrible blablabla.

(Passenger 2 gets out book, thus giving the other person the book-off. Passenger 1 stops talking.)

the shit

The best. Without "the," it has the opposite meaning. "My teacher is shit" = bad teacher. "My teacher is the shit" = the greatest teacher.

Man, this weed is the shit! I can barely feel my feet!

Man, this weed is shit. It tastes like oregano.

(verb) the shit out of

To do something to a great extent. If you (verb) the shit out of (object), you REALLY (verbed) it hardcore.

The Tampa Bay Rays beat the shit out of the New York Yankees last night. The score was 15–2!

Rachael Ray really baked the shit out of that pie. That motherfucker was tasty as hell!

Haley Joel Osment really saw the shit out of those dead people in The Sixth Sense.

the spousal we

The opposite of the royal we, instead meaning "you." Used by your significant other to get you to do something.

We should clean the bathroom today.

this guy knows what I'm talking about

An expression used to diffuse responsibility for an unpopular statement made in a public setting. Typically used to imply complicity or collusion on the part of an unwilling stranger.

You: I mean, really, who hasn't made out with a run down fat chick in a moment of drunken desperation.

Crowd: (Silence)

You (smiling and pointing to a random guy in the crowd): This guy knows what I'm talking about.

this is actually happening

Phrase used to highlight an awkward or unbelievable event. Depending on the context, it can be used as a positive reinforcement to encourage the behavior, or as a negative reinforcement to discourage the offender.

(Three hot women approach a man and his friends in a bar and ask if they can join them.)

Lucky man: This is actually happening.

(A friend in a group starts to complain about others in an irrational and mood-ruining manner.)

Another group member: This is actually happening.

thrift whore

1. A person who shops at many different thrift stores, thereby often finding wonderful deals.

She's a total thrift whore, so she has all these cool, one-of-a-kind clothes.

2. One who feels the urge to brag about every single piece of crap they find at a thrift store.

Becky is such a thrift whore. She found a flying horse for a dollar—big deal!

throw under the bus

To sacrifice some other person, usually one who is undeserving or vulnerable, for personal gain.

He'd throw his mother under the bus if it'd mean he could beat the rap.

thumb lashing

To be reprimanded via text messages on a mobile phone, as opposed to a tongue lashing in person.

I was supposed to take her out for dinner but I stayed with my friends at the bar, and boy did she give me a thumb lashing!

Tiger's wife mad

An anger so great you want to find the item the person you're angry at cherishes most and beat them with it.

Chris was so Tiger's wife mad at Joe that he grabbed Joe's Wii remote and beat the shit out of him.

time vampire

Something or someone who sucks your time like a vampire sucks blood.

My computer broke again. I spent all night working on that fucking time vampire.

tired high

A state of altered perception brought on by a lack of sleep.

When he started to hallucinate he wasn't sure if it was the weed or if he was just tired high.

TiVo time zone

A time period that lags behind real time; created by letting the TiVo build up enough to skip commercials.

Jim watches all the Raiders games in a TiVo time zone and turns his phone off to avoid any spoiler texts.

tl;dr

Acronym for "too long; didn't read." Used when you see text that is too long to bother reading.

tl;dr . . . why dont you give up on your unabridged edition of War and Peace *or at least stop emailing it to us?*

TMI

Acronym for "too much information." Used when you get way more than you need or want to know about someone.

John: I have mad chafing on my balls.

Frank: Uh, TMI.

to your point

Phrase used to contradict another person's ideas while making it feel like you have agreed with them.

Her: I don't think we should see each other anymore. You're just not there for me emotionally, and I need more than that.

You: To your point, I think we should limit our relationship to strictly sexual, and I look forward to that. I'm glad we agree on this.

toe up

Wasted beyond belief by an illegal substance of some sort or by alcohol. Also "tore up."

Yo, man, I'm gonna go to that party tonight and get so toe up you won't recognize me!

toilet mummy

When someone is so concerned about toilet seat germs they cover the seat with half a roll of toilet paper until it appears as if it has been mummified.

I was going to use that stall to drop a deuce, but somebody left it looking like a toilet mummy.

tongue typo

What happens when you know perfectly well what you want to say but it comes out wrong.

In a horrifying tongue typo, I accidentally called my boyfriend, Marc, by my dad's name, Mike, while we were making out.

toolbox

A mega tool; a boy who thinks girls worship him when they really want to vomit on his shoes. Also "tool kit."

Matt is not just a tool—he's the whole box of tools, a complete toolbox.

tooth sweaters

When you go for a day or so without brushing your teeth, and the texture in your mouth feels like your teeth are wearing fuzzy little sweaters.

Cara: Does anyone have gum? I forgot to brush my teeth this morning, and it feels disgusting.

Pete: Oh, you've got tooth sweaters?

toothpaste hangover

The effect that makes everything taste disgusting after you brush your teeth.

Ugh! This orange juice tastes horrible thanks to that gosh-darned toothpaste hangover!

touch base

To make contact; to cover all the possibilities. Comes from baseball, where the runners need to touch the base to make a run legal. Mostly used by asshat salesmen and contractors when they want to talk to you over the phone to see if you're interested in something they have for sale, usually around dinnertime.

Telemarketer: I'm just calling to touch base to see if you need our crappy product/service.

Me: No, fuck. Leave me alone.

traffic Tetris

When you come to a stoplight and make the conscious decision to avoid getting behind a dumptruck or semi and opt for the lane with ten vehicles instead of just two so you're sure to move sooner when the light turns green.

Oh no! Now I'm stuck behind a tow truck. I need to brush up on my traffic Tetris skills.

traffic Tourette's

The uncontrollable urge to scream obscenities at other drivers who infringe on your space (whether real or imagined).

Mark: That @#$% can't drive worth @#$%!

Jay: I see your traffic Tourette's is getting worse.

traffuck

Peak-hour traffic, or any general traffic that slows you down.

I'm late for work and stuck in traffuck.

trailer fraud

When a trailer misrepresents the movie it advertises. When you view the actual movie, you realize that the trailer has nothing to do with the narrative, characters, or plot.

J. D.: Boy that film sucked!

Gil: Yeah, what the fuck did we just watch?

J. D.: Dunno; the trailer looked good.

Both: trailer fraud!

transaction

The sex you get from a cross dresser.

Man, that girl I met at the bar last night was actually a dude, but it's okay. I got me some sweet transaction.

tri-sexual

Someone who will try anything sexual.

Person 1: What's your sexual preference?

Person 2: Hey man, I'll do anything. I'm tri-sexual.

trusticles

The balls to trust someone in a difficult situation, when the failure of that trust would result in injury or financial loss.

I know I got my law degree online, but we're family. Show me you've got some big trusticles and let me defend you in court!

truthiness

The truth one wishes or believes to be true, rather than the actual facts. Coined by Stephen Colbert on *The Colbert Report*.

That Fox News report didn't have all of the facts, but it had a certain truthiness to it.

TV face

A condition in which a person's face becomes too relaxed from staring at the same thing too long (such as when watching TV). Symptoms include: open mouth, dropped jaw, eyes glazed over, and occasional drooling.

I don't think he heard a thing I said. He has total TV face right now.

TV stoned

Completely deaf and blind to everything but a favorite show on television. One who is TV stoned is unlikely to answer the phone, speak to anyone, or do anything except sit and watch. He or she is also likely to be irritated or react badly if one tries to talk to him or her during that hour or the duration of consecutive favorite TV shows.

Sorry, I can't get Bill to come to the phone. He's TV stoned at the mo. Call back after the show is over.

Twitter bang

Hooking up with someone to whom you've spoken fewer than 140 words.

Sarah: How did you meet Rafael?

Jenn: At some random friend of a friend's party. I'm not sure even how we ended up in bed. We pretty much met over brunch the next morning.

Sarah: Sounds like a Twitter bang!

twitterpated

Complete and immediate infatuation with someone or something that occurs with the onset of spring; giddy excitement rooted in the physical. From the Walt Disney movie *Bambi*.

Ask Marie about her new army boy. She's so twitterpated she can barely talk.

typeless

So astounded that one cannot type. The writing equivalent of "speechless."

Dad, that story in your email message left me typeless!

typeractive

Overly talkative on emails or text messages.

Man, Emily should get a job. She's been text messaging me every two minutes. And there are ten emails in my inbox from her. She is way typeractive today.

U

UDI

Acronym for "unidentified drinking injury." The random bruises, aches, and pains one picks up when drunk.

Greg: I'm pretty sure I broke a finger playing cards last night. Wtf?

Oliver: Sounds like a UDI to me.

unbrella

An umbrella turned inside out by forceful wind.

It won't keep you dry—but if you want to, you can stand under my unbrella-ella-ella.

underboob

Cleavage visible from the part of the shirt that covers the bottom of the female breasts.

If that is not a deliberate underboob, I don't know what is.

unlightening

A process of "learning" something that makes you feel dumber.

The conversation I had with my blind date was so unlightening that I practically fell asleep before the salad course.

unprotected sleep

Turning off your alarm clock and immediately going back to sleep, risking not waking up for a job, class, or other daily task.

I'm lucky that I didn't miss my final exam after having thirty minutes of unprotected sleep.

unsult

An insult disguised as a compliment, originating from *The Simpsons*. The disguise can be very obvious or very subtle.

From The Simpsons*: "Hey, Lenny, it takes a lot of courage to wear suspenders while you're not performing in the circus."*

Urban Dictionary

A site where users attempt to mock and explain everyone and everything in life under the guise of cynical quasi-intellectualism. It should be both noted and ignored, embraced and dismissed, laughed at and revered.

Urban Dictionary shows us we're all just a type, no matter how hard we try to escape or deny it.

Urban Dictionary cover-up

The act of scrambling onto UrbanDictionary.com to quickly find out the definition of a word (usually when used over texts or IM) to cover up the fact that you do not know the meaning of that word. Commonly abbreviated to UDCU.

Person A: yo dude, that jam was live last night.

Person B (after UDCU): yeah, that was a pretty cool party.

urban farmer

A person who constantly plays FarmVille and acts like they know everything about a real farm, but all they do is live in the city, sit at a computer, and at a certain time need to stop what they are doing to farm their imaginary crops.

Carly won't shut up about her stupid farm and throwing sheep. What an urban farmer.

U

V

vacation amnesia

When you come back to school or work from your vacation and you can't remember what you did before your vacation.

Andy suffered from a bad case of vacation amnesia when he went back to school and couldn't remember what he had been learning before.

vaguebook

To give an intentionally vague Facebook status update that prompts friends to ask what's going on. Possibly a cry for help.

Mary is: "wondering if it is all worth it"

Mark is: "thinking that was a bad idea"

Mylie: Have you talked to Mark? He's vaguebooking again.

Angie: I wonder if he's back with Mary. . . .

Valentine's Day

The reason so many people are born in November.

I was born in November because my parents celebrated Valentine's Day.

Vatican roulette

The rhythm method of birth control, the only form of contraception endorsed by the Catholic Church.

Well, the pope says condoms are out, and the pill is born of the fires of hell, so get out the calendar, Baby, 'cause it's time for Vatican roulette.

V-card

Virginity. All virgins have a "V-card" until they "cash it in" for sex.

Guy 1: Jason spent the night at some girl's place.

Guy 2: Did he cash in his V-card?

vegetarian

A bad hunter. Someone who survives by consuming not food, but the stuff that food eats.

The vegetarian was forced to subsist on slower prey, such as the broccoli and carrot.

verbal handcuffs

When someone won't stop talking (usually about a subject you have no interest in). The talker verbally forces you to stand there and listen, even though you have given many clues that you have checked out (i.e., vacant stares, looking at your watch, checking your phone, answering in short, one-word phrases).

Haylie: So then I realized my cat really likes Meow Mix more than Friskies, but only if I mix it with Fancy Feast.

Brynna: (Stares blankly)

Haylie: Unless of course it's chicken livers from 9Lives; Snowball loves that. It's her favorite.

Brynna: Uh-huh.

Haylie: Of course, on her birthday I give her the good stuff: real tuna!

Brynna: (Looks away, thinks, "Fuck me, verbal handcuffs. . . .")

violent agreement

When two people think they are arguing but fail to realize they actually agree.

Ross: This arena is bigger than the old one.

Morgan: Not much bigger.

Ross: It is bigger.

Morgan: Barely; hardly enough to notice.

Ross: It's definitely bigger!

Morgan: But NOT MUCH bigger!

Chris: Uhhh, guys? You're in violent agreement.

virgin ears

A person who has been only marginally exposed to sex, drugs, and profanities, and doesn't have a tight grasp on reality.

In order to protect his virgin ears, little Billy used earmuffs while Daddy told his buddies about what he did at the bar last night.

virtual Friday

The last day of work or school in a workweek due to taking time off for an extended weekend.

I'm so glad I have Thursday and Friday off for Thanksgiving. Even though today is only Wednesday, it's virtual Friday!

VOCD

Acronym for "volume obsessive-compulsive disorder." A psychoneurotic disorder characterized by an obsession or compulsion to adjust the volume on the television to a "perfect" number, such as 15, 20, 25, etc. The affected person suffers extreme anxiety or depression through failure to adjust the volume perfectly or by witnessing an "imperfect" number, such as 9, 16, 31, etc.

I hate watching TV with Joe. His VOCD is so bad he doesn't really even pay attention to the show because he's so focused on the volume.

voicejail

The loop of options in which you get stuck when trying to navigate your voice mail.

I tried changing my phone greeting, and I got stuck in voicejail for five minutes.

voluntold

The exact opposite of volunteering, where someone assigns you an unpleasant task.

Coworker 1: I hear you got a transfer.

Coworker 2: Yeah. I didn't want to, but I was voluntold.

vurp

A burp laced with a little vomit; usually occurs when you've had one too many and it has become difficult to distinguish between the two.

I made it through the whole night without vomiting; not including vurps, of course.

waffle crapper
A chick so hot that you wouldn't care if she walked up and crapped on your waffle. In fact, you'd probably welcome it. Coined by Adam Carolla.

She's no waffle crapper, but I'd hit it.

wait, shit
Something you say after realizing what you just said or did was idiotic or bad.

Dude, my dick is so big that if I laid it out on a keyboard it would go from A to Z.

Wait, shit.

wake and bake
Waking up and, while in bed, immediately smoking the "prepacked" bong that is sitting ready to be smoked on your bedside table. Can be used to describe any situation where someone smokes within one hour of waking up.

I'm becomin' a bit chronic these days, like wake and bake every day and shit.

walk of shame

When a woman leaves the home of a man (quite possibly one she met the night before) in the early morning hours—hair sticking out in all directions, makeup half gone, with her undies in a pocket or her purse.

After a night of partying and excessive drinking, Cheryl woke up God knows where with an unknown man beside her. In a fit of regret, she gathered her belongings as quickly and quietly as possible and crept from the man's home to do the walk of shame.

wallet threat

Reluctant act of pulling out one's wallet as a gesture of willingness to pay for a meal one assumed was a treat.

Royce: Mike, put that thing away; dinner is on me tonight.

Mike: But it's so expensive.

Royce: Dude, seriously, chill out with the wallet threat.

wank

1. British slang for masturbation.

There was a guy in the park having a wank in the bushes.

2. A discussion without purpose or substance that often involves pretension and bullshit.

Then the entire conversation degenerated into complete wank.

wanker

A British term for one who masturbates. Commonly used as a general insult.

That wanker cut me off in traffic!

wanksta

A contraction of "wanker" and "gangsta," used pejoratively to label those who purport themselves to be gangstas but who are simply posing as such.

I saw Baz wearing all his bling yesterday, and his most thuggin' gear, threatening to duff people up. He really is a total wanksta.

wantrepreneur

Someone who thinks about being an entrepreneur or starting a business but never gets started.

Bill is such a wantrepreneur—always talking about starting a business, but never getting there.

wapanese

A derogatory term used to describe anyone who is a fanatical follower of Japanese culture. Often finds the Japanese culture to be superior to any other culture, and takes great pride in showing off a new word or new words learned from anime or manga he/she has translated. The term "wapanese" is often misapplied to any person who watches anime, or Japanese cartoons.

Wapanese munch on imported Pocky and wash it down with a bottle of Pocari Sweat.

web shy

Unwillingness to expose one's thoughts, feelings, or identity on the web, knowing that doing so means freaknobs from Baton Rouge to Bangladesh will know everything about you.

Robert: Jeez, Paul—you need to get with it! You should create your own website, post your picture, do some blogging about your beliefs, and generally trumpet yourself and your innermost thoughts via that there Internet.

Paul: You kidding me? I am waaaaaaaay too web shy for any of that!

weiner cousins

Men who have had sex with the same woman/women. This is a bond that can never be broken.

We're weiner cousins now, and that means we're closer than brothers.

what the actual fuck?

An expression of surprise or confusion used when "What the fuck?" is insufficient to convey the magnitude of the situation. The increasingly flippant use and associated devaluation of the query "What the fuck?" has necessitated the creation of this more heartfelt derivative.

Meg: Have you seen Russell's beard yet?

Jason: Yeah . . . what the actual fuck?

whatever

Word used to admit that you are wrong without actually saying it, so the argument is over.

Man, whatever.

whatever lifts your luggage

Synonymous with "whatever floats your boat."

That gay hooker that the renowned homophobe hired when he went overseas is not cute at all; but hey, whatever lifts your luggage.

whateves/whatevs

A noncommittal, nonchalant answer to practically any question, usually accompanied by a shrug of the shoulders.

Sarah: Do you want to go out with me tonight?

Margaret: Whateves.

wheels of steel

Record turntables, often specifically (but not necessarily) Technics SL1200 series turntables, noted for their steel platters.

This is DJ Hyper manning the wheels of steel tonight.

when the economy picks up

Common beginning or ending to a sentence. It can serve to:
1. provide an excuse for why one has not yet done something.

There's no point in looking for a job until the economy picks up.

2. suggest a vague intention of doing something later (similar to how Spanish speakers use the word "mañana").

I'll start my business when the economy picks up.

W

3. add minimal credibility to an idea that is a pipe dream.

Unemployment levels will go back down to the levels they were in the late 1990s when the economy picks up.

whilin'

Too harsh in manner, tone, or behavior.

She be whilin' and she don't understand why no one likes her.

whip

1. Someone who has their significant other under their thumb/control.

Jonno couldn't make it—he's out with his whip!

2. An expensive, stylish automobile or motorcycle.

My dad let me drive the whip so I can take my girl out tonight.

wi-five

Mix of "wireless" and "high five," hence "wi-five," or wireless high five. A high five that doesn't involve physical contact. Normally done over a long distance where a real high five isn't possible.

Ian (yelling across the room): Dude, that was teh pwnz. Wi-five, brosef.

wigger

A pejorative term for a Caucasian kid who mimics the language, dress, and mannerisms of black ghetto kids.

Wigger: Yo, bizzle, you best step off mah bread!

Suburban white girl: Didn't you get that do-rag at Hot Topic? And why are you wearing a FUBU shirt?

Wigger: Yeah, well . . . you know that's how we do. . . .

Wii elbow

Similar to tennis elbow, pain in one's arm (particularly around the elbow) caused by too much Wii tennis (or, possibly, not enough regular exercise).

I got a horrible case of Wii elbow from all that Wii tennis yesterday.

wikidemia

An academic work passed off as scholarly yet researched entirely on Wikipedia.

An A on my English paper? That's a fine piece of Wikidemia!

wingman

Someone who goes along with their friend on a date so that when their friend picks up the hot girl the wingman gets stuck with her ugly friend. A very noble job, and guys usually switch off wingmen at different clubs.

Aight, man, I'll be wingman this time and fall on the grenade, but you owe me big time.

word life

Interjection meaning "I swear to you on my life what I tell you is true." It was used by rappers in the early '90s to mean "I promise."

I'ma send you cryin' to yo' mama after I mess you up! Word life!

W

word receptacle

The person on the receiving side of a one-way conversation.

I couldn't get a word in edgewise. She kept talking to me about her shoes, purse, and how her best friend just got dumped, and I just stood there being her word receptacle.

word vomit

Something you said that you really didn't mean to.

I told Robin that I saw Mike with some girl at the movie theater last night. That word vomit just came out of my mouth.

work avalanche

So much work piled on you or your desk that movement out from under it is nearly impossible.

Hey—pour me a drink! I worked up quite a thirst digging out from my work avalanche to get to happy hour.

work hot

A person who may or may not be hot among the wider population but is the most attractive person in the set of people you work with, so you lust after him/her.

Oscar: So this new girl at your work—is she hot?

Liam: Hell yeah . . . well, I mean she's work hot.

work mouth

A form of self-censorship often practiced in work settings to avoid using offensive or cuss words. Does not apply to all professions. For example, musicians and construction workers have no need for it. Typically includes cuss replacements you learned from your grandma. Can also be used in the company of grandparents, teachers, preachers, and others who disapprove of cussing. Potentially embarrassing if accidentally used at parties or in the company of your drunk friends.

(At work)

My boss: Did you just say "fuck"?

Me: Yeah, sorry. I forgot to use my work mouth.

(At a party)

Regan: Did you just say "fiddlesticks"?

Me: Yeah, sorry. I still have my work mouth on.

work paralysis
The inability to get work done because of its large quantity. Similar to writer's block, but applies to all work with a deadline.

The stack of paperwork had reached an all-time high, and I was hit with work paralysis.

worked
Getting beaten very, very badly in a competition of skill.

If you went one-on-one with LeBron you would get worked.

working hard or hardly working?
Funny play on words used by successful management types. Can be paired with finger guns for the ultimate combo.

W

Supervisor: Hey Joe! Working hard or hardly working? Hahahaha.

Joe: Hahahahaha! You're the best boss ever!

workout impostor

People who walk around in workout or gymlike clothing to give the appearance that they have worked out or gone to the gym, or are planning to work out or go to the gym, when in reality they have not or are not going to. They usually do this to make themselves feel better about their physiques, or to seem like they are physically fit, when in reality they have done nothing.

Look at that girl in the Nike shorts, Under Armour shirt, and Asics sneakers wearing a ponytail. She is totally a workout impostor. I didn't see her at the track or the gym at all today.

writer's crap

Derived from "writer's cramp," refers to a stage when one is only capable of writing utter crap.

That story was horrible. I think she's got a bad case of writer's crap.

WSD

Acronym for "write shit down," a popular method of organization that works equally well in one's personal or professional life.

Dude, you don't need Ritalin. Just use the WSD method. Trust me, you won't forget things anymore, and you'll actually get them done!

WWJT

Acronym for "what would jesus text."

Do not pass text messages that ruin other people's reputation. Stop and think, "WWJT?"

X-rayted

TSA rating for airport naked-body-scan images.

Hey, Sarge, check out these X-rayted pics that I scanned this afternoon.

yard sale

1. The evidence or remains of a catastrophic accident or wipeout, in which the victim's belongings are scattered or spread out across a large area (resembling a traditional yard sale).

The U-Haul trailer fishtailed into the oncoming semi, then the median strip was a yard sale.

2. To fall while skiing or snowboarding and leave a trail of gear behind.

That two-planker is having a yard sale down there.

yarr!

A word often used by pirates whenever they have experienced a loss or pain.

Yarr! My pirate's booty has been stolen.

yawn pong

A game played by tired people. In short, one person yawns, and then the other person does. Should the original yawner yawn twice before the second person yawns once, player one has one point.

We played twelve rounds of yawn pong last night.

yellow listed

Someone who does not wash their hands after urinating.

You may want to double up on the hand sanitizer after shaking hands with Edith; she was yellow listed last week.

yellular

The loudness one adopts in response to a bad cell phone connection in the misguided hope that talking louder will improve the connection.

I'm so embarrassed. I went totally yellular at a restaurant last night.

yestrosexual

A formerly homosexual person (usually male; for females "hasbian" is preferred) who is currently in a relationship with a member of the opposite sex.

Allen: Knut used to be dating Brad, but now he's dating Liz.

Derek: Sounds like he's another yestrosexual.

yoink!

An exclamation that, when uttered in conjunction with taking an object, immediately transfers ownership from the original owner to the person using the word, regardless of previous property rights.

Though I cherished my automobile, I had to purchase a new one when my second cousin came up from behind me and politely exclaimed, "Yoink!" while taking my car keys.

you lie!

The classiest way to respond to anyone you disagree with.

Obama: There are also those who claim that our reform efforts would insure illegal immigrants. This, too, is false—the reforms I'm proposing would not apply to those who are here illegally.

Joe Wilson: You lie!

you wastin' my minutes

A phrase used when someone says something stupid and you don't feel like listening anymore. Similar to "Bitch, please."

Bitch, you wastin' my minutes.

your mom

Comeback expressed as an intended slight on a maternal figure. Often serves as indication of the end of a conversation.

Darren: That is one very fat farm animal.

Jeremy: You're a fat farm animal.

Darren: I'll show you a fat farm animal.

Jeremy: Your mom is a fat farm animal.

Y

your other left

Sarcastic phrase uttered to the directionally challenged to make them aware of their error.

Doctor: Raise your left hand.

Directionally challenged guy: (Raises right hand)

Doctor: No, your other left.

you're probably right

A phrase used to ease the blame and embarrassment associated with getting something wrong.

Jack: I know that girl. Her name is Cindy.

Joe: She's my neighbor. Her name is Angela.

Jack: You're probably right.

YouTube attention span

Significantly decreased attention span brought on by the use of YouTube. Whereas normally ten minutes is a short amount of time, YouTube turns it into a cinematic experience.

Jill: Watch this video!

Jack: Okay . . . wtf? Ten minutes? That's way over my YouTube attention span.

YouTube degree

A bachelor's level certificate that people award to themselves after they have deemed themselves to be experts in a particular field of study by watching various instructional and how-to videos on YouTube.

Ben: Whoa! That is NOT the correct way to put on cologne! You spray and then you walk into it.

Joey: Okay, and since when did you become the expert on all things cologne?

Ben: Since last spring, when I got my YouTube degree in cologne management.

YouTube moment

A moment or short event when you wish you had a video camera with you. The video equivalent of a Kodak moment.

It was a perfect YouTube moment when Chris tripped and fell down a whole flight of stairs.

YouTuber

One who spends so much time browsing YouTube videos that they have metaphorically taken root, in the manner of a potato or other root vegetable. A couch potato of the new millennium.

Shawn: Oh, man, I haven't showered in three days. I've just been sitting at my desk with a bag of chips and watching YouTube videos!

Kody: Dude, you'd better watch out—you're about to become a YouTuber.

zipper-spark

To dry hump while clothed.

Oh man, John wanted to zipper-spark with Susie so bad behind the bleachers at the junior high school.

thanks to the following Urban Dictionary authors, whose definitions appeared in this book and are some of the most popular on urbandictionary.com.

Adam B.	Disgruntled_in_SJ	CarlInLB
Bottom Ford	JJE	aelso
flaxypoo	UliDarling	Madison R.
bandit bob	DB	uniquenowflake8
Tom Cohen	Somechickwhowritescrap	Devin84
thebetterfriend2	spektralx	The Pigfarmer's Grandson
The Middle Man	Eric M.	Jeremy H.
the Italian Cowboy	Jeremy W	viking maiden
Jevanyn	Lucky Luc	Kevin Black
ThreePts	papa_squat_0516	tommypjr
VoytekTumanov	wozdog	Dawn D.
stevezoid	Adam T.	lunar shadows
20th century boy	Paradox Q.	the_elder
catrap	TeacherBitch	Sonoma County Dave
Innocent3	Marc H	Theako
Courtney H.	tiki	PhoenixFanatic
Zero Of Da Star67 Boys	breezy-licious	Didda Tinkle
andytheslash	Nikki F.	TallGreg
rebl girl	Dommie phantomjack	Boggler
waylonisthebombdotcom	Daveycakes	butterfingas
Bran Man	ITALUS	adk132
El Don Diguidi	wecomefromstars	brand x
David Hawaii	Deepthoughts	ashenannigans
Funk Naz-T	Tootybug47	PanamanianWhiteMan
Domestic violins	Toad	Liz's mom
Cory N.	1Spectre4U	Unconcious
KGB	the booniepepper	nullswitch
Tony J.	sircasey	JenThe80'sFan
OliveBinItaly	boaluta	eculaugh

Pablo2342
haydizzizzle
Eidetic Memory
CourtJ
Sanzone
Kevin F.
PaulieJr
52tease
Da Nastee One
Tha Funkinator
Ya Kno
bratina
Lord Andre
KingOfTheStreets35
Delongpre Dannon
no one
Low Clef
SVS
Kahoki
j5_teh_evil
KrautKontrol
Wine Chick
James D.
Katymc
Robocoke
pilaman
Herb N. Dictionary
Prof. Wetwang
Chiefnutz
santa clothes
Flora
David T.
jscilz
Cap
John
anthubc2010-
    perfectionist_par
marcata

TrueKore
The Canadian
    Information Minister
Silky Smooth
Beaqon
FemmeFatale
LEVIATHAN1000
Smitty
wanking_at_gunpoint
Anna
AtlantaHoopla
joel
sutch
oogens
Joe C.
billy_fizzle
belikecat
Whitney R.
NotKnown2
katydid
brunette22
Melissa
Mark N.
Courtney T.
IceWarm
DaSnoopinatorFoSho
defying gravity
Taliesinson
Devoniscool
Alan K.
LoneWolf275
manateehunter
Crispin Cheesey
Margaret S.
caroline s.
Alley's Mom
Matt
Sean Boots

Mighty J.
Boomer
Ella123
LimaUK
Wanderlust
hngryDavy
pigpen23
quarterlife crisis
Elgebar
raindove
Marco R.
K1dCuervo
urbanAstrophysicist-
    WannaBe
RFenyman
Dr E Short
matkillah
abdoo mustafa
j. christ
grlwholvd
nikkiandmorganarecool.
Sir Neville W.F.G. Mariner
Basic Thug
Loogaroo
TheWireIsAwesome
TC99
Sam M.
harlan500
Turnspike
westfalia
rach BFD
CPD
Al
Angelacia
Handmaid
Lesbrarian
BMF 2010
bryan

rzaragoza
Geoff A.
Edward in Oil City
Do.g
Sirann
Jock T.
honkhonkin
youdontsmellbad
Telin
Andrukas
jecole14
12_mrwebster_12
sammich
Jamiecam
AKA bobby
A. Danish
Max M
PunTiff
violentfemme
ExtraFine
Mikep
Foggy
Thejuicer
jigsawz67
Mackster66
Andy
daphnia_b
Holly W.
offulspellir92
miss crazy sexy cool
MoonCricket
HHH
Mr.Juan-derful
JakeStar
meadow soprano
phatguy
Zennon
Jeremy D

Michael E.
tatm artista
MoLo36
Juan "The Garrioch" Hefe
Gimster
LehFreakshow
SkynSea
marc ipsen
Final Attempt
Albert
EJL
Buzz A.
baked_12
Nemon23
jokepoacher
kymcleod
DaStrangla
daveeee
James F.
Joel M.
NicoleN
Fish Fooood
Lincoln "THUG LIFE"
The original ARDvark
Phuturephunk
tchotchotch
Chris_K
Naegling
alison
nuzach
FreshPrince369
The C-Man
Mopsynator
vot
Mktkm27
Tricia
Stuart L.
naterooni

gooddave
mattalicious
Eric M.
deez nutz81
Michael F.
Jessicka.
Nick McD
cosmo
TRON 2.1
FreeCottonCandy
JoeyJr.
Taggz
bun
I Like Bread
Rosie
harry's girlfriend
erieee
Oprah
Nick D
RoninRogue
The Rope
Chaz W.
mkic0n
Brown Sugar
Kimmy K.
Mosen
HB Brother From
    Another Mother
frag142
DerAffenkoenig
Mark S.
roofette61
The Return of Light Joker
Fox64
Roni E.
David U
dunderscott
David E. K.

Greg

Mario R.

weave

Twigman

shaniqua2

phorks

Picabo192

DjLimitless1

Joshtown

Craig 119281

Hamfry

Harlo37

Dominick

freaknsweet

zfunk

a random choch

Grothefro

BMOUNZ

Vowtar

I Work 99

Elizabeth B.

Diego

neochin

Acquiesce42

shinney

theunknowngl

your mom

JT Basher

B&E

Hone

Ellen T.

Chrissy12321

Shen

steve-f

Lydia

m0

Cephiroth

DOAREK

tkearns

Bushbrother

stikjock

Exploding Boy

Solstice B.

Thanatos_A

Jerry8675309

Screw farmville

Adam L. B.

kingnuthin

Kickkc

eus091142

bert2

John F. O.

KaTe.

Joy Rising

ae123456

Super D

Aeronius

Honorarius

Elena

cammie B

matt d.

Professional Drum Driver

sick bastid

nope

DoctorA

Marimar

Ofcourse

Zee'Krey

Big South

grimfish

Our Van Ankle

Y-Dawg!

tagz

ShangstaGangsta

Boone W.

Markspal

T

Ilovehobbies

Brosef17

Set the Controls for

slinger91

Notorious JJM

BvO

Sheri P.

Mr. John 2

charlie Studtaco

Ron's Cookies

toast455

aoc

angry social worker

Oletha

wouldaben

The Grammar Nazi

Jeffrey

Mattster12345

Antony

Mudshovel

extra_pickly_pickles

mysterius man

wendyrocks

sheepyone

el

TheGreekMind

ThatsTooBad

D.K.Y.

Rob

Hunt E.

DerrtySouthBaby

Hyperman036

Ryan

relaxfrancis

BiggyG

Tailspin

Alpine M.

SnaggPDX
mattblackHQ
frickafrack.
david f
Smiledriver
JLLee
Brett B.
a1b2c3d4e5
L.K Winters
chittydog
ShadowInTheNight
Chris.G
AbsolutValu
themudking
Jacob S.
The Other Joey
Edgar Spelling
Bird Turggler
miggie
Andrew85
Travis
Shaun G.
ScottySlave
USMale
Kyle M.
lightbulb
Foof
Universe24
tf
Amanda SBG
kevin
Gleeky
Weed Whacker Wally
Reni W.
kris t.
NocturnaLucid
ralphWookie
Dawn

AiRsTrIkE
brooklyncat
AK47 & Bowlerina
csepulv
NGX
Bloo
David F.
steel girl
David H.
PeeBee
j.r.
Jim S.
angrywhiteflag
JDrummer86
Snarky Puppy
Antonie L.
Harvey W.
Big Derek Big Time
HudsonDuster
biscuithead
Logan H.
WHUDDDUP
magic_8ball
Oooglie Booglie
naknumm
hurtadaa
Matthew G.
Rollie H.
bobmcd123
sharkfoot
Bobalicious Brown
XileLord
quicksilverdime
Am B. Dextrous
NightRoseK
malmix
Rydo
grimridersuxcock

jxb
Maven
C.K. Dexter Haven
Bigtexxx
tortuga azul
Vebond
iPutMyWordInYou
shoewhore
CFallon
Jachmaninoff
andrew m
Poop Stain Barney
Hepcat
Nathaniel E.
Laura
President Warren G
drew s
bonnie
Phil
pmpknqueen
glasmodiar
evil_gumball
eswqc
Cimmerian Southpaw
McVillain
Yebeka
DrCyclops
ignor
Fat Tony
johnne-boy
Bradshaw
jdcftb12
ElinorG
WastingDaylight
savantwaler
floorfly
Zorgithatoob
abbayyo

mpfl
Bob Box
spmack
pennymj
Jigga Jaime
JalWilly
Katy
B. S.
kayakbeat
Arman J.
danpinole
Lie_Detector_411
daniel h.
fletchlives
Jeff A.
Nathan M.
Bec
em bee kay
malendras
DinoDavid
GFVFTL
Randori
Mr M. Ister
voltages
daphniab
Stampy
Glenn T.
Murderbox
SweetTart2K
Just Put Italian
BlagoGal
wordsbywilson
Jeff D.
mheartstar
blackdeathmessenger
Skylighter
Casey
Andrewsky

DarthVerso
Sid B
smokina fatone
Daylorb
8675309
Chauncey B.
rjv
Hollywood Swinging
binary132
localhoax
nihilistic0
Samick D.
anonymous
Russell C.
kidAndrew
Fat Finger Tony
horsecock_jenkins
pow3rslave
Rtrock
Katie Oh!
Salvdor
rich, happy, soul-less,
    robot
El Mexigringo
Ryan OVB
Delaware Mike
yaaqov
Bryan G.
haroldhendu
sam b.
sandyland
JrMint
Zig Awesome
b34r
HecklnDecalr
zachfree
Jescati
DonBito

NekoPocky
mrtoodles
Kaatisu
Qeqeneq
Laura M.
Teresa M.
kneb
Rossatron6000
Jace555
Laurent H.
mandawoowoo
Crapholio
JROA
Roy 2019
ACNY
pose2pose
gmoney63
medicalmechanica
Broman in NY
DJ Akay
Jason
Kon T.
angel c.
chaniqua
Orchard
minky
ty
Vince L.
illicit_fun_owns
shambone
Aaron S.
archlich
SchwarzerWind
Cyclone
Darrel C.
Ronnie J
T.
Guiseppi P.

Andrew L.
BTheWordMaker
Ryan-ALR
KingdomO
dAnIeLa
ShoKill
dejaflu
shilohfire
MrMOSCRU
g-money
Palidori
Nigel W.
tnear
gabe t.
chemiosmotic
uwg
Nutty J
Craig M.
dave3:16
sally in the car
teedoff
Stytches
BADDAZONER
Emmsey S.
hapahacker
Monkdunker
James P.
TFT1974
mellow_harsher
OnipSemaj
Natale S.
happyfish
Marc L.
Pail/Concussed/Crevice
Caitlin+Courtney
nomes
Buzztell
zooa

ashamalee
icwish
Spirit of Truthiness
Daddyman
Spiv
Caroline
Desiree1990
Jeul
zipwolf
iGoTmAiPad
Chris B.
the dez
Nemesis
Cap'n Sweaty!
april1
Frank B.
Cynyc
AEAizzle
Rachel L.
Funeral in Fame
Master Bates
Cara and Sloopy
sandraooh
T.R.S.
Xiki
Lygreen145
Ted M.
ckarlo
Theropod
TimS.
mollygoodhead
the ppl's champ
Surface Tension
Maximum C.
zerrlok
Endymion
Edmond L.
evilhighpunkin

SoccerKid3310
K- K- KATIE!
David T.
Darkwise
Joe S.
dj_monged
Charles U. F.
Dave
MDermy
hex_ten
AliceInUDland
Cara D.
JL Patrick
Nick And
wordlife18
Dan A.
billinom8s
Carrie N & Adrienne V
speedworxs
Philosophistry
DisgruntledJoe
JudyD
buzzub
attifinch
redbelt
hockeyguy071
k and D sessions
RocketPower10
Dolphin_X
Wayne-K
Bungalow Bill
Gmagnum GJA
hyperexcel
sir smokalot
0xxMillyxx0
mrmcd
nubluva
american-wife

LynZ M.
Bloodbath 87
hbdanny
Cale Dempster
Jog DMC
John G.
The Tree7635
Larry C.
Icky Thump
katamos
Anonymous
Greg H.
Jake'n'Bake
Mica M.
Tom's Mugshot
sky
do.g
mini_man543
NCdubMixer
ganjer9
Dan04
pixelfairy
SemperLieSuckah
Jonny_B
snarkette

sweetnsassi
Tarrasque
jeteye
Ardouche
dmcormond
BynoT
DocGonzo
klacebo
TheShrewKing
Satan
DigNbubbles
MR. B3NNY
Squigman Fraud
imav
bunn28
Dara L
dsfswdfsf
Upper Class Twit
The Cabal
Nobody0000
Laurie
whoa there dude
jacaranda
Hackermom
js1993

Therightwordsareeverything
Cybercass
Jasrags
krapnek
Jesse K.
lilyrandall
Tchotchotch
Irish Dave
Erik
jervis_star1
Rogue Sun
Francis Ford Dopella
cloverhays1
Tom N.
thaley
SeaOrland
Rothdaddy
/>/_//\/<^/\/
HG ColdDawg
HockeyUSA72
WarpFactorFive
Char H.

aaron Peckham was a freshman in college when he started Urban Dictionary, a parody of dictionary.com with a twist: everyone was welcome to write new definitions. Soon Urban Dictionary garnered hits—and new definitions—from around the world. Its millions of visitors and authors made Urban Dictionary into the world's dictionary, with more than 6 million definitions describing current events, pop culture, and the newest slang.

Aaron reads urbandictionary.com from the San Francisco Bay Area.